Images of
Survival

Images of Survival

ROBERT A. LLOYD

DODD, MEAD & COMPANY
New York

The author wishes to thank the following publishers for permission to reprint from the material indicated.

Alfred A. Knopf, Inc./Random House, Inc.: THE TECHNOLOGICAL SOCIETY, by Jacques Ellul. EDUCATION AND THE NEW AMERICA, by Solon Kimball and James E. McClellan, Jr. WORK, LEISURE, AND THE AMERICAN SCHOOLS, by Thomas Green.

The Viking Press, Inc.: MR. SAMMLER'S PLANET by Saul Bellow. Copyright © 1969, 1970 by Saul Bellow. All rights reserved. BETWEEN PAST AND FUTURE by Hannah Arendt. Copyright © 1961 by Hannah Arendt. All rights reserved.

Charles Scribner's Sons: CHARACTER AND OPINION IN THE UNITED STATES, by George Santayana. "A Clean Well-Lighted Place" from THE HEMINGWAY READER.

Holt, Rinehart and Winston, Inc.: THE POETRY OF ROBERT FROST edited by Edward Connery Lathem. Copyright 1928, © 1969 by Holt, Rinehart and Winston, Inc. Copyright 1942, © 1956 by Robert Frost. Copyright © 1970 by Lesley Frost Ballantine. SELECTED LETTERS OF ROBERT FROST edited by Lawrance Thompson.

ISBN: 0-396-06783-2
Library of Congress Catalog Card Number: 73-1658
Printed in the United States of America
by Vail-Ballou Press, Inc., Binghamton, N.Y.

To my father
my teachers
my students
and my sons

Acknowledgments

IF I were to acknowledge all literary debts, all the borrowings of experience which contributed to this book, the list would be long. I will confine myself to mentioning three books. The first, James Agee's *Let Us Now Praise Famous Men,* showed me that one can be honest without being dull. The second, *Experiencing Youth,* by George Goethals and Dennis Klos, broadened my sense of what is on some people's minds, and suggested in what ways I might be of use to them. The third, Schiller's letters *On the Aesthetic Education of Man* (translated by E. M. Wilkinson and I. A. Willoughby) portrays a view radical at the time (1795) and still relevant. Schiller's language is slightly remote, his categories of thought are somewhat foreign, but he chews on the same problem—how to see individual and society in a single way that is best for both—and uses the same weapons—synthetic thought and honest attention to the experience of being individual and human. The organization of his essay, too, is clearly nonlinear. Certain kinds of ideas must be circled about and entered from a number of different directions.

The list of people for whose conversation I am grateful is also long, as is the span of time over which our talk was talked out. Many of my ruminations started eighteen years ago in speaking with George Miller, Professor of Psychology at Harvard, when, for a spring, I was a student of his. I doubt that he remembers me, but he managed to give me a real sense of confidence in my thought. Skipping to more recent years: Eric Schroeder, late of Cambridge, honored me by arguing with me; Guy Hughes of Milton Academy shared enthusiasms; Harold Owen of Phillips Andover dared share experiments; and David Tyack, Professor of History and Education at Stanford, taught me much about the disciplines of educated discourse. I owe special, undefinable thanks to Gerald Shertzer, of Phillips Andover, for rich conversation over the years. In certain ways, this book is another product of the sculpture-woodworking shop which he and I share.

For specific textual criticism my first debt, because she had first shot, is to my wife, Sue, whose sensitivity to pretentiousness and balderdash helped weed out much nonsense. Carey McIntosh, of Rochester University, and James McIntosh, of Yale, provided many concrete, helpful criticisms. Jim, from his lively familiarity with Thoreau, transmitted sympathetic energy, as he has over the years. Carey played devil's advocate and slipped several skillful points under the guard of my complacency. At greater distance and somewhat more formally, important suggestions by E. M. Wilkinson, of London University, and by Van Cleve Morris, of the College of Education at the University of Illinois, have been incorporated.

The Trustees of Phillips Academy, Andover, should be

cited for generously providing the time and the means without which this book would not have been written.

Finally, I commend to you the patience of the Publisher.

Tinmouth, Vermont

Contents

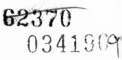

Images of
Survival

1 Introduction

To have the chance to speak (or write) to an audience of many people is dislocating. At least I find it so. One has to cross over so many borders to foreign territories, from the local to the large, from the named and familiar to the anonymous and unknown, from the safe and semicontrollable to the dangerous and accidental, from the society of friends and enemies to a land of innumerable, faceless, pallid gossips by whom one cannot tell whether it is better to be noticed or ignored. These are difficult crossings, but the most painful is from the personal and private to a presumption of general social usefulness, from concrete, idiosyncratic perceptions, as they occur and as they are remembered, to an expectation or hope that they will be valuable to a large number of people.

If I describe the delight I experienced as a child picking wild strawberries on a certain New Hampshire hillside in

1940, a hillside long since grown over to pine, yet still a hay-
field in memory—light breeze softening the glitters of sun
through the patterned movement of elm-leaf shadows, the
texture on my bare knees of grass, twigs, and moss still cool
with morning's dew, the growing ache in my back as I search
and gently detach the sparse, hiding berries, the ever-present
temptation to eat instead of pick balanced precariously
against anticipation of wild shortcake made with heavy, un-
pasteurized whipped cream from a neighbor's cow, all in the
peace of a summer away from school, floating in an infinite
period of time in which I could shape my life as I wished
from moment to moment, meal to meal, day to day—you
may enjoy the description, you may begin to share the personal significance with which I have invested the experience,
but you can never, never "have" that experience, or rather,
be possessed by it, in the same way or with the same energy.

On my part, no amount of hard work, good will, poetic
skill, communicative technique or indirect persuasion, logical or rhetorical argument, threats, forcefulness of personality, clarity, exemplary behavior, even love—nor, on your
part, of desire, attention, curiosity, envy, fear, or again love
—none of these can bring the power and shape of that experience across the space between us. The experience cannot
be repeated, planned for, nor in any way be made to happen. It cannot be reached by moral or religious striving, nor
induced by drugs. It cannot be touched by any measures of
intelligence, physical well-being, social adaptability, moral
rectitude, psychological development, or artistic talent. It
can be the source of neither pride nor shame. In a word,
such an experience—not publicly available—is *useless*.

Yet somehow I must convince you that such events, along
with our personal investment in them, comprise the most
significant history of our education, more important than
our intellectual achievement, athletic prowess, social adaptation, or any other gestures we may have learned to make in

the direction of the many. My message starts with a paradox: the most socially "useful" person is one who has been pointed least in the direction of social usefulness and most in the direction of openness to the immediacy, uniqueness, importance, and energy of his private, personal experience. In a different metaphor, the most valuable person to society is he who has been allowed to develop in his own terms, around his own center, integrating in his own way the unique, dynamic totality of his experience. This process, in broad terms, is what I mean by *private education.*

Three central questions, or sets of questions, rush in upon this assertion. The first set has to do with the person. If we allow him to think that his most important education lies in his private experience, what is to prevent him from tending toward asocial, if not antisocial, behavior? If we let him sit on the vine, ripening in the sun of a private euphoria, how are we ever going to induce him voluntarily to pick himself off the vine, step into the world of work, and make himself part of our organized society of consumers? What will prevent him from rotting where he lies? Will he not isolate himself from all others? Will he not end up in a powerless solitude with nothing to do, no place to go? Maybe he will attempt to organize others to take life easy and threaten the existence of society—even to the point of waging a guerrilla war against it? Finally, if he has been born poor, how is he ever to improve his share of the nation's wealth and power?

The second set of questions has to do with society. How can a large, complicated, expensive social organization, penetrated with technological perceptions and assumptions, continue to function if its human components are not primarily defined, shaped, and trained efficiently to fit into the necessary roles and stay there? If we do not encourage the young person to feel, as a large part of his motivation, an intense loyalty to our society at large and its galaxy of social organizations—loyalty based on respect, gratitude, and strong involvement—how can we ever persuade him to make the often unpleasant, and sometimes fatal, sacrifices necessary for its continued survival and growth, or more immediately, for his own welfare and the welfare of his family? Isn't our nation only a society, only a civilization as it is *organized*— as its members work together, divide and distribute labor? Do we not see a fierce privatism even now destroying our society, both in the complacency of our self-centered, pleasure-seeking bourgeoisie, and on the other hand, in the idiocy of our drug-abusing, bomb-blasting radicals? Even if we grant that our society has problems, failings, sources of instability, aren't these all the more reasons to try harder to *make* the system work? Where else can our society turn for its survival if not to our children? More concretely (and crassly), since as a nation we spend a great deal of money on education in all its forms (fifty to sixty billion dollars per year, now), is it not a moral imperative that education be directed toward our children's eventual return on that investment?

The third set of questions bears more directly on the relationship between person and society. Doesn't there *in fact* exist a mutuality between them, a give and take which, if properly organized, results in the best for both? Hasn't it been demonstrated that the happiest person is he who has come to terms with social demands, has modified himself, adapted his goals, his desires, his pleasures to fit as nearly as possible the opportunities provided by society at large? And that the best society is that which contains the happiest people—comes closest to providing them what they want? Further, aren't person and society two terms in a single equation, inextricably related, objectively influenced by each other at all times? Isn't this a truth that would be stupid, wasteful, *dangerous* to ignore, especially in educating children, "the future members of society"? Aren't we convinced that the healthy psychological development of a person occurs largely in the company of other people? Is not the soli-

tary person nothing, a vacuum in a vacuum? Finally, aren't
we sure that a person's spiritual well-being, his sense of personal worth, the deepest bases of faith and trust in himself
grow from the stability of the way he sees himself as a
human being among other human beings? Isn't it the ultimate *duty* of our society to try to provide this well-being,
this richness of faith—the solid ground on which a person
can meet, participate with, and accept his fate? In sum, isn't
it impossible, rather than simply subversive, to postulate the
existence of "private experience," much less suggest that it is
the source of any value?

These are strong questions. I feel their force, yet to me
they share a flaw: I do not know who is asking them. In fact,
I suspect that they do not come from a person at all, but
from a piece of mind, a partial perception that many people
share—and enjoy the sharing of—which is drastically incomplete. The gist of their argument goes: (1) "We" want the
child to be as healthy as "we" are; since he won't become
healthy if left alone, "we" must help him. (2) "We" are a society, and unless the child joins us, our society ("we") will
die. (3) If "we" *make* the child a healthy member of a
healthy society, child and society will be healthy. Our suppositions and actions are therefore virtuous, *quod erat demon-
strandum*. In the same breath, each of these questions suggests
and implies a goal and a way of reaching that goal. Each
begs its question. Each is, in fact, rhetorical and ideological.[1]

The observation that ideological arguments are circular is
not new. Neither is the observation that argumentative circularity is more obvious—and more irritating—to a person
who does not accept the initial premises than to one who
does. The latter is probably unaware of the tautology. What
does seem to be new—as the result of many factors which,

----

[1] An ideology, to me, is an organized, abstract, fixed system of thought
implying that certain ways of thinking and behaving are acceptable and that
others are not. Rhetoric is simply the clothing of ideology.

during the last ten years, have far outrun their explanations
—is that many young people are so irritated with the circular ideology of our society, especially as they encounter it in
our educational system, that they are joined in war against
it. The basic assumptions do not fit theirs. The curious and
sad thing about their reaction is that it, too, is ideological.

There seems to be a historical human compulsion to fight
the fire of one ideology with the fire of another. Who gets
burned? Who else but the individual, private person? It matters little whether we speak of the atomic flames of Hiro-
shima, the magnesium flames of Dresden, the gas flames of
Belsen, the napalm flames of Vietnam, or the sudden hot
rush of gas exploded in a research laboratory in Wisconsin:
the man buried in the rubble is just as dead, the all-too-fa-
miliar victim of incomplete consciousness, of the mind crip-
pled by ideology. Victim and victimizer have both been destroyed by the compulsive systematization of thought, our
hasty human confusion of order with truth, against which
the dead can bring only silent witness and beyond which the
ideologue cannot even suspect his error.

Of these crimes against the individual it is clear, to me,
that we cannot excuse the rigid ideology of the conservative
and his conspiracy of complacent violence; nor equally, the
frenetic ideology of the revolutionary and his conspiracy of
cataclysm—the blown bank and the blown mind. Probably
they need each other: who else needs either? But how about
the ideology of the center, the conspiracy of conformity? The
rhetoric of the "silent" majority, bringing the message of social utility and conformism, is our constant companion,
more pervasive even than the transistor radio. Perhaps that
is why we do not hear it. The ideology of education, which
powers our conventional reactions to individuality, penetrates all reaches of our diverse educational system: our
schools, our families, our occupational activities, our media,
our conversations, our forms of recreation, our language—

even the most intimate aspects of our lives are informed by the normal, the systematic, the pseudo-reasonable. It matters little whether one's privacy is invaded by a psychology of sex or pornography, the invasion has occurred. Even if we manage to control the arrogant power of the military-industrial complex, we are left with the much more insidious and thoroughly dangerous technical-ideological complex. At this point in history it is difficult to tell which is the worse fate: to die by sudden fire or to succumb to the slow, silent burning of decay in the quality of our global, national, urban, suburban, and rural life. Even in the furthest reaches of wilderness the careless bubblegum wrapper bursts the illusion of solitude, and suggests that for the individual there is no escape from the machine, the social "scientists," and the money-makers. "The system" will trap him in one way or another.

> The individual is in a dilemma: either he decides to safeguard his freedom of choice, chooses to use traditional, personal, moral, or empirical means, thereby entering into competition with a power against which there is no defense and before which he must suffer defeat; or he decides to accept technical necessity, in which case he will himself be the victor, but only by submitting irreparably to technical slavery. In effect he has no freedom of choice.[2]

Again:

> Granted that the development and growth of the individual is a worthy ideal of any society, it is our contention that its realization depends upon the nature of the conditions, social and cultural, within which he must live and work. This being so, *self-realization is to be seen*

[2] Jacques Ellul, *The Technological Society* (New York: Vintage Books, A Division of Alfred A. Knopf, Inc., and Random House, Inc., 1964), p. 84.

*not as a goal but as an unearned dividend arising from
certain structural connections in the public world.* Our
real concern, consequently, is that the structural discontinuity between family and locale on the one hand and
the great superstructure on the other is creating an environment in which commitment, in its public, objective
sense, is becoming obscure. We are fearful that technological superiority, material prosperity, the institutions
which ensure their achievement, *and the cult of the individual* have become ersatz goals in American civilization.[3]

Or again:

Education, even deliberate education, is always concerned with: (1) socialization, (2) cultural transmission,
and (3) the development of self-identity in the individual. . . . By "socialization," I mean the process of induct-
ing the young into society's adult roles, as these are defined structurally. By "cultural transmission," I mean the
process of learning, adopting and adapting those beliefs
and values that provide some degree of rationalization
for the social mores and practices that the child learns.
By "the development of personal identity," I mean two
fundamental but distinguishable requirements of education. The first is the demand for some meaningful partic-
ipant roles in the contemporary community; the second
is the need for a sense of identity with some historically
developed community.[4]

All these voices belong to men critical of contemporary society. The first is the most pessimistic: in his view, the technological view now controls the human will to the degree

[3] Solon T. Kimball and James E. McClellan, Jr., *Education and the New
America* (New York: Random House, Inc., 1966), pp. 237–238. Emphasis
added.

[4] Thomas F. Green, *Work, Leisure, and the American Schools* (New York:
Random House, Inc., 1968), p. 148.

that he sees no hope at all for the power of the private, idio-syncratic person to survive. The second speaks of the individual's freedom only as an "unearned dividend"—an aristocratic experience floating above his competent involvement in technocratic labors, a matter of personal fortune, good or bad. The last sees the system expanding, more or less benignly, to encompass greater freedom for the individual, but insists on the absolute need for systemic blessing.

What am I supposed to tell my children? If I believe Ellul, then I should say: "O.K., Ben—and why don't you listen, too, Seth and Tom—here's your choice. If you want to be yourself, fine, but you will be destroyed by society. If you don't want to be destroyed by society, become a competent technocrat: destroy yourself." If I believe Kimball and McClellan, I should say: "Boys, don't pussy-foot around. Shape up, find your niche, do your job well. Maybe you will find a few moments, some day, that you can call your own. They may be kind of fun." If I believe Green, I should say: "Sons, things are working out slowly. Get your training, get your job, earn your living. Meanwhile, don't think that this is the whole picture: you have to find ways to make sense of your behavior; you have to belong, I mean really *belong,* to your community. Oh, and read the classics. They were great men, then, great men. You'll find it all begins to make sense after a while, maybe in thirty years or so. Meanwhile, we'll try to take care of it for you."

Not much of an offering. I would be ashamed to make any of these statements to a child. I will not make them to mine. My refusal is not a matter of my awareness of the damage such statements do, their inherent cynicism. Nor is it simply their repugnance to me—the desperation of the first, the hard-nosed philistinism of the second, the scrawny fatalism of the third. Nor the fact that I cannot look a child in the eye and make the words come—that to do so I would have to become an embarrassed apologist, a dirty-handed middleman for the system. No, my ultimate inhibition is that they are *untrue*. They have little or nothing to do with growing up and learning how to live. Children know it. I know it. Their knowledge is private; so is mine. I must respect the private knowledge they have been given and have developed, each in his own way. If I don't, it will all blow up in my face. Bullshit begets bullshit.

The social voice, enticing with dreams of communal reward, threatening with nightmares of isolated despair, drives us toward the rape of our uniqueness. Is there no ideology of privacy? Is there no system of thought with which we can fight off the groping fingers of conformity which seek to rob our personal integrity for its social worth? Is there no rhetoric of privacy with which we can exorcise the Joneses from our minds and the minds of our children, and shame them and ourselves into an independent self-respect?

I hope there is not.

In solitude, we need a private ideology, but we do not need a public ideology of privacy. We need a private rhetoric, a language with which to speak to ourselves in silence, but we do not need a rhetoric of privacy, new ways of making contemplation noisy. To paraphrase Nabokov: all happy people are more or less dissimilar; all unhappy ones are more or less the same.[5] I hope—and that is all that I can do —that we are not so lost in the mazes of our technological-ideological consciousness that we can no longer freely live in our personal universes, enjoying our growth as we enjoy the glimpses we catch of the powerful, unique privacies of other souls, their growth, and their richness. A simple thing, and in these times, very difficult.

It is all I want for my children. If I can, it is all I would like to give my students. Whatever capacities for it I possess I will defend with my life, because they *are* my life.

[5] He is reconstruing Tolstoy, at the start of *Ada*.

2 A Self

THE place to begin is before the beginning, not in order to find the precedent cause of what we are as people, what you are as a person, but to find how we began to think of ourselves. We were before we began to think we were. What were we, then? How did we come to see ourselves at all? In what ways is my view of myself and you different from your view of yourself and me? If you sense the difference, maybe we can begin to talk.

I see myself as a nomad—a monadic nomad. I am singular, independent. I travel, I move around, I change environments. Physically, I travel less than I used to. Mentally, more. I have found that geographic travel—which I still enjoy—is not necessary for a change in my environment, and actually hampers movement in many ways. I have found that I can even change occupations, as well as points of view, and that these changes are more challenging, more demanding,

more stressful than the rigors of driving a car, of adapting to
new climates and time zones, or of fitting in with new patterns of life. Yet with all the changes, the challenges, the new
delights and unexpected brutalities, semisuccesses and apparent failures, I find that I have not lost a sense of self, a center. Like a racing pigeon, I know where home is.

A man I know has been trying for five years to determine
how the pigeons do it. He thought, at the beginning, that it
wouldn't take long. He already had a hypothesis of which he
was pretty sure. It was simply a matter of isolating certain
inputs to the bird's central nervous system, shutting them off
one by one, or in combination, and finding which depriva-
tions caused the bird to fail. He has blindfolded them,
deafened them, subjected them to anesthesia on the trip out
to the release point; he has loaded them with magnets to
confuse any sensitivity they may have to the earth's magnetic
field; taken them out to sea, far beyond any familiar land-
marks; totally thrown out of whack any built-in organic
clock on which they might base a solar or a celestial naviga-
tion; subjected them to erratic and violent motion to upset
any inertial guidance system they might have. None of the
birds has shown any significant hesitation: they may fly a
half-circle or so, and head right for home. My friend is beginning to consider ESP.

Only one thing: the birds refuse to fly in the dark. They
land and wait till morning. Probably to avoid collisions.

I can't explain to you how I know where my home is, either. I don't mean a geographic location, you understand, a
specific environment, or a special group of people—
something outside me. I mean my home inside me, my
"self." It is not a place, a point, a hideaway to retreat to in
times of stress. Nor is it a state of mind, a feeling of repose.
It is neither a mood nor an idea. I can think about it, as I
am right now, but I cannot think it into existence. No, *it
thinks me into existence.* It precedes me, my every sensation,

my every action, my every word, my every thought. Even
when I think about myself, it precedes that thought, too. It
is always *behind* me: it must always be a place of darkness
because it lives behind my eyes; it is the silence into which
my ears play their music and can be heard; it is the expansi-
ble space in which a furniture of ideas can be arranged and
left in storage. Whole experiences organize themselves
within it, fade into forgetting and sometimes, after periods
of blankness, blaze into memory again. Into its darkness I
drop the ingredients, and a problem is solved, an insight
achieved, a synthesis made fact—I don't know how. It is a
night within me into which I call for help, and help always
comes, sometimes immediately, sometimes more slowly than
I can bear. Into it I deposit my dreams, and from it the
nightmare calls its warning. It is within me and yet is large
—so large I can never reach its limit. It has no face, no
limbs, no shape: it is neutral, indifferent, judicious, always
fair. Yet it is alive. It is at all times impersonal, and yet it is
I, my person, my home. When I have to go there, as Frost
says, it has to take me in.

> "Yes," said Mr. Sammler, "that is a very nice way of
> putting it, though I am not sure that there are many
> people so fine that they can feel this light weight of
> being so much more than they can grasp!" [1]

Maybe. I would say there was choice involved, although
difficult choice. Certainly one's self is hard to think about,
lying there beneath every thought. And there are many,
many aspects of our contemporary culture which, by pretending either that this self does not exist, or conversely,
that we can know what it is, tend to isolate our thinking—
and all that follows our thinking—from our sense of its

---

[1] Saul Bellow, *Mr. Sammler's Planet* (New York: The Viking Press, Inc.,
1970), p. 225.

being always present yet always beyond our reach. We tend
to assume that our thinking is self-sufficient, and like to forget our forgetting. Consciousness, like culture, works by
selective feedback—amplification of choices made—and focuses its eye on the object of its attention: who needs the
weeds that have been discarded? We only occasionally remember that we are not just creatures of our culture. What
we have bred in the hothouse of thought is still meager compared to what we have been given, by nature, to begin with
—before the beginning. We cannot, in fact, throw anything
away from us. Weeds or not, all sifts into the hidden self,
where it may be beyond recall but exerts unremitting control on our growth.

We are vulnerable. Mind and larger, hidden self are neither immortal nor unresponsive to the apparent orderings
and disorderings of the world outside us and around us. But
of all the possibilities of pain implicit in our existence, there
are two which cannot be endured. The first I have hinted at:
that we become separated from our hidden selves, embrittle
our minds, and isolate our thoughts from the generosity of
our own natures. The second danger follows from the first: it
is death. Not the death which nature gives—also in her
generosity—but the violent, physical death that we give ourselves prematurely, driven by isolated consciousness and by
the compilations of a culture which nurses us toward our
mutual and self-destruction: war, self-inflicted disease, eco-
logical disaster.

The issue is our survival.

The path to our survival lies in the person, in you: in
the defenses you can develop against those cultural forces
which try to tear your consciousness loose from its moorings
within you and to deprive you of your hidden wealth of self;
and in the easy momentum of growth you can develop, a motion toward complementary, simultaneous enrichment of
your consciousness and of its far side, the silent darkness

within you. Travel with will and pleasure, but never lose your home. Our culture, as you travel through it, can at times blind you with its light, and in the eyeball pain of its glare two temptations seem almost reflexive: either aggressively to become an indistinguishable part of that light—a gleaming, glittering flare; or to close your eyes and hide in your own darkness. Succumb to the first and you lose yourself and die. Succumb to the second and you lose the light of your consciousness. Even the dumb pigeon knows better than to try to fly at night.

A Survival Manual, then.

I don't mean something like, "How to Survive in the Wilderness with Three Matches, A Razorblade, and Two Feet of String"; nor "The Big City on Four Dollars a Day"; nor "Money in the Mirror: Ten Easy Steps to the Career and Income of Your Choice"; nor even "Face Your Maker: Five Paths to a Happy Death-Bed." Yet I cannot get away from the insight that the many examples of self-improvement manuals—from the banal to the biblical—all share the realization that **important changes in a person occur primarily because of changes in his perception, changes in how he sees himself and his universe.** If you see yourself in a new way, immediately you start to become a new person: the change is organic and total. If you see the universe in which you live in a new way, immediately you start to become a new person: the change is organic and total.

Thinking lies between the self hidden within and our perceptions and actions as we relate to whatever lies outside us. Thinking inhabits a world that lies, in its entirety, between two unreachable extremes. In one direction away from thought, toward the center of the self, lies the ideal: that perfection which has moved entirely away from the contingencies of the outside world and of personality, and is free to be unified. As Plato has Socrates say: "Since I am one, it is better for me to disagree with the whole world than to be in disagreement with myself." [2] In the other direction, pointed outward to the world, lies the real: the perfectly contingent, absolutely nonrepeating source of stimulation, always elusive and dangerous—or at least indifferent to our safety—which at one and the same time threatens us with instant death and supports our life. It is well to remember that at all times this world, to which we ascribe "facts," "actuality," "objectivity," "evidence," and even occasionally (in our madness) "rationality," lies outside the world of thought no less than does the ideal. The outside world will always be in the process of disappearing and appearing: it never stands still.

Survival is concerned with the real rather than with the ideal. And so, in what follows, although much will seem to be just thinking, it is always thinking pointed in the direction of the world: how do we perceive it, how do we act into it, how do we survive with it? What follows are thoughts, not ideas: perceptions of the world and actions into it, not retreats toward philosophic truth. We see by daylight.

In the first chapter which follows I give you thoughts about some basic ways each of us is defined, the nature of solitude and isolation, and the conditions of individual survival. Among other things, in this chapter I will attempt to give more substance to the idea of privacy which I mentioned in the preface. The second chapter discusses various ways of understanding the relationship between individuals, their communication, and thereby the conditions within which they can help each other. The third chapter discusses the relationship between the individual and larger social groups, and begins to develop a perspective on the educational aspects of this relationship and on the quality of individual survival in a changing society. The fourth chapter consists entirely of concrete examples of educational rela-

[2] Plato, Gorgias, 482, as quoted by Hannah Arendt in *Between Past and Future* (New York: The Viking Press, Inc., 1961, copyright 1968), p. 220.

tionships, and the final chapter, when you get there, will speak for itself.

In addition to this progression, which is outlined for your reference in greater detail in Appendix I, "A Structural Paraphrase," there is another kind of organization to the material which follows. In different contexts, in different minds, the different sections are attempts to say the same thing. Each chapter, each section of each chapter is another attempt, another try, another wave on the beach which at its height changes the pattern of sand and slips back. There are thoughts in the second chapter which pull back to the first: opacity, for example, informs the idea of the sensory shell. Concrete examples in each case speak to what precedes as well as to what follows: my experience with the Eskimos, for example, has as much to do with solitude as it does with companionship. More drastic still, you can, if you wish, read the Appendices first.

As each wave breaks, the shape of the water and the shape of the sand uniquely change, but the water remains water, the sand, sand.

3 Solo Flight

THERE is a pivotal picture, a first perception, which defines, in terms as absolute as I can reach, our predicament. In certain ways we are perpetually isolated from our environment and from each other. Even the most cursory knowledge of physics and physiology makes this clear:

Item: what lies within our skin-volume is drastically different from what lies immediately outside it. Usually we are not aware of our insides, but even when we are—when we are sick and feel our internal malfunction, or when we are well and simply wondering—we cannot *see* our insides. But even if we go to the extreme of cutting up a cadaver, the immediate and obvious fact is that the smallest scalpel stroke reveals something new, something vividly different from what we saw before.

Item: our continued existence consists entirely of transfers of energy through the surface of our skin-volume, either from outside to inside, or from inside to outside. For example, food and excretion, heat and chemical transfers, our reactions to gravitation, the external transfers of physical momentum, and most significant to us, the informational reactions of our nervous systems.

Item: these transfers, without important exception, involve distinct and drastic changes of state in the energy transferred. The food pumped through our arteries is different from the food we eat, as are the substances we excrete; the heat of our bodies, bound inside our solids and liquids, becomes for the most part vaporous and radiant when released; the mysterious, pervasive energy of the gravitational field becomes particularized within us, affecting our sense of balance, the physical relationships and functions of our internal organs, even the success of our adaptation from a prehistoric four-footed stance; the contained, controlled reflexive momentum of arm or leg changes into the free motion of objects we push or throw—even into our own free movement; and in our sensory nervous system, the impingement of light, the pulsations of air pressure we call sound, the mechanical forces of touch and felt texture and temperature, the chemical variations of taste and smell, all these and others are changed into the still mysterious electrochemical information of the cellular nervous network.

Item: our perceptions, thoughts, feelings, and actions are more closely related to—if not identical with— the operations of our nervous system, in its

physiological structure and function, than to any other parts and/or systems of our physical structure. Simple fact: much contributing evidence, no evidence to the contrary. The question of the identity of our subjective experience of life and the objective operations of our bodies must remain a question: the two points of view from which the two kinds of knowledge grow can never coincide. The man who holds the dissecting knife cannot dissect himself, and the man who wishes to understand himself cannot achieve that understanding with a knife.

Item: seen in a broad way, our nervous system is organized, both structurally and functionally, in two distinct parts: (1) a thin, exterior shell, one or two cells in thickness, comprised of sensory receptors and motor effectors, best understood as a mechanism of differentiation; and (2), within this sensory-motor shell, a large central volume best understood— despite its incredible complexity and differentiated structure—as a mechanism for connection between the receptors and effectors of the shell. The cells of the outermost shell, as they impinge on its surface, are totally independent of each other and have no anatomical or functional connection with each other. In the case of the sensory—incoming—nerves, their function of differentiation is further amplified by the fact that, for the most part, each cell responds more strongly, and with more definition, to changes of stimulation—to contrasts of energy—than to the constant, nonvaried impingement of energy. Over any period of time, short or long, all that exists in this shell is a very large number of cells in various states of excitation, or viewed more abstractly, a very large matrix of points, each of which, measured with some approximation, could be called 0 (not-firing) or 1 (firing). Each point is changing from a 0-state to a 1-state, and back again, at a different rate of speed. To add to their differentiation, some fire when stimulated, others fire when not stimulated. And of course, each cell is responsive to one kind of stimulus and not to others. Difference piled on difference, distinction on distinction. Do you understand? In themselves, these stimuli have no relationship to each other aside from being different. Together, they form no pattern, assume no order, make no sense. All this shell does is change its state, in some (partly understood) response to the changing state of our physical environment. In fact, we must say that whatever lies within this shell, it is isolated from all else, all that is other than us, by an impenetrable barrier which translates all impinging energy into an always changing, very complicated and enormous quantity of what, to any mind,[1] must be considered nonsense. That is, it cannot be understood except, indirectly, by reference to some further, larger amount of information that exists somewhere else outside (or within)

[1] As opposed, of course, to any brain. I can hear the objections of those who have spent their lives understanding the relationships between stimuli and their internal effect, attempting to make sense of what I am here calling nonsense. I hereby challenge them: let every single one of my sensory cells be connected to a light bulb so that when it fires, the bulb flashes. Let these one hundred million or so bulbs be distributed at random (to order them in any way would be to have reference to information—either their origin or destination—lying outside the shell here delimited) over the wall of a room. Let a record be kept of a five-minute sequence of the flashings of this array. I give any scientist as much time as he has, and as much equipment as he needs, to tell, on the sole basis of this information, precisely what I am seeing, what I am hearing, what I am smelling, what I am tasting, what I am touching (and where), what position my body is in, and the state of my digestion—so far as I am aware of it—during that five-minute period. The chances of his success are much, much less than the probability that the punishment machine of Kafka's "Penal Colony" ever existed, although the relationship between the two situations is very close!

this thin shell.

Within the volume of the nervous system, separated
from what lies outside us by this sensory-motor filter,
occur whatever processes with which we organize
the chaotic, nonsensical data of the peripheral shell
—by bringing bundles of nerves together, allowing
them to interact with each other in regions, ampli-
fying the messages of some and suppressing others,
connecting different regions structurally and opera-
tionally, allowing some of the data to make permanent changes within us, organizing and diffusing
our actions in mediate response, and relating all of
these to the other, the nonsensory and nonmotor parts
of the system: the autonomous functionings of heart,
diaphragm, digestive system, glands, and more cen-
trally, the lower, more primitive sections of our
brain, which seem to be more closely connected with
our emotions.

*At our periphery, where we are in contact with
whatever lies outside us, we are so constructed as to
react to and produce a very large number of contrasting and changing stimuli; the continued operation of
the periphery can provide only more new information. At our center, where we enjoy the processes of
connection, we are utterly isolated, separated, shut
off from what exists outside us by this shell of nonsense.*

Whatever we think about what lies outside our
bodies, whatever we perceive, whatever feelings we
have about the outside world, and whatever actions
we may take toward it—all of these thoughts, perceptions, feelings, and organization of actions take place
only within our bodies, in form, structure, and kinds
of energy entirely different and separate from what is
outside us. Whatever we see, whatever we perceive

out there, we can be sure that that is *not* what is there. Whether we are enjoying the gentle fall of a spring shower as it brings a secret life to a dried and dormant nature, or watching in horror the actual, violent death of a fellow human, we can be sure that neither the rain nor the blood is falling in our head. And conversely, whatever we mean or attempt to show in our actions—including those which, like speech, are intended to communicate—we can be sure that our statements and our actions are *not* our intentions. Statements and actions are external, while our intentions remain within us. *Any transaction between inside and outside, in either direction, involves a complete change of state.* The more objective we become about what we are internally, the more information we have about how we function, all the more are we forced to the conclusion that we are, in fact, totally "subjective," forever bound within our own skins. Strange paradox!

We are left with many questions. If we accept not the general truth of these facts, but their continued, inescapable, and concrete trapping of our every internal experience, up to and including our most sublime and profound thoughts and feelings, within our bodies, we are forced to contemplate the possibility, and perhaps the necessity, of despair. How can we trust any sense or meaning that the universe, out there, has for us, in here, if at the same time we know (in precisely the same way that we know everything else that we trust of knowledge) that sense, meaning, *and trust* are all part and parcel of the same question? We are first forced to recognize that the question of our trust, like our sense of truth, is inescapably a matter of individual, solitary, and unique decision: in this our freedom is absolute. Second, since the question of trust—in precisely the terms I have described—is always renewable, our commitment one way or another is at all times open to reexamination and change. In this, despair and trust are equally vulnerable.

Item: when we make detailed comparisons between people in terms of their structure and function, described above, we find that they are most alike in their peripheral mechanism, least alike in their central functioning. The range of response and relative reactions of the peripheral nervous system are, for the most part, standardized over the entire human species, while the varieties of thought, perception, feeling, motivations, and forms of action are enormous. The most precise agreement we can reach is that two stimuli are different, distinct—in fact, that they are stimuli. The farther we attempt to proceed in the direction of understanding their organization, in thinking about them, in establishing their meaning, and in acting in response to them, the more we diverge from each other and are forced to recognize our divergence. In those external relationships which have particularly to do with other people, the paradoxical perplexity of our situation is further heightened: the only parts of us which we share in a standardized way and which operate in a predictable fashion—our peripheral stimulation and capacities to act—are just those which consist of endlessly varying, changing, fluctuating, nonsensical data which for each of us alone are absolutely nonrepeatable, much less sharable with another person. Whereas, in those parts of us where we begin to organize and make sense of our peripheral chaos, precisely there, where we *want* to connect, where we *want* to share

our meaning, where we can know and feel what sameness is, we are the most unique: there is, in fact, no
objective basis of comparison between us. Within
even the simplest statements we make to each other
begin to float unknown quantities and shapes of
meaning. In short, if we pay any attention to each
other at all, we know we are isolated and must remain so, and that when we speak to each other, it is
over a great distance, in a great silence.

**Item: Finally, given our present knowledge of the
significant variables in the physiology and psychology
of the human being—a knowledge which can only
become more sophisticated—we can say that the
number of significantly different internal states of
being that are possible for each of us, in our responses to stimulation, in our initiation of action,
and in our free choices between trust and despair, is
infinitely large.**
N. B. the following known variables:
1. The nonrepeating, nonrepeatable variety of the
   total field of stimulation.
2. The number of receptors and effectors, perhaps in
   the hundreds of millions, and their sensitivity to
   minute changes of stimulation.
3. The size of the central nervous system (nine to ten
   billion cells), a large percentage of which is
   "freely" organizable: highly responsive to variations in internal and external stimulation, and capable of a large degree of amplification—small
   changes can easily lead to big changes.
4. The variable ingredients of memory: minute and
   multiple changes in cellular circuitry and chemistry.
5. The large number of distinct inputs from the au-

tonomic nervous system.

6. The large number of possible variations in the total or general electrical and chemical state of the brain.

7. The highly variable states, permanent or temporary, attributable to illness and diseases, known and unknown, affecting all the above.

8. Genetic variables affecting all the above.

All of these factors, separately and combined, indicate a *very large number* of possible organizations, which can change rapidly. In these terms, each of us is infinitely rich in potential, in the number of contrasting "states of mind" he can entertain, and in his abilities to perceive and act differently at different times.

Our internal wealth so described serves to define two important ways in which we are further isolated from whatever lies outside us, or at least certain areas of that universe with which we often try to identify. First, each of us individually possesses more possibilities of internal, organized states, and these can change much more rapidly than any agreed upon social, economic, political, or religious system as we so far understand them. Even the complexities necessary to describe the organization of our entire nation are small compared to the complexities each of us contains within him. That is, we can never match our internal states even momentarily—much less permanently—to any social organization except by the gross suppression of information about ourselves, or on the other hand, by a highly flexible interpretation of what a social organization is—flexible to the point where we must wonder whether, aside from the operational (and essentially mechanical) pressure toward agreement, it is organized at all.

Second, we are isolated from both social and broader, natural organizations in comparative predictability. Our large internal capacities guarantee our low predictability, even to ourselves. I challenge you to predict, for example, what your thoughts will be and what your feelings will be two minutes from now. It is just possible that you can force yourself to say certain words to yourself at that time, or picture certain pictures (for some reason). But as to their meaning or your total awareness of them, these you cannot make dance to your tune. In fact, *they* are *your* master. Understand, I am not saying that meaning and awareness are whimsical, flighty, or fickle. Just unpredictable. I can throw a stone into the air and predict that it will fall, but I cannot make any such predictions about my internal states. In this respect the stone and I are forever foreign to each other. You and I, at least, are peers: we enjoy the same degree of wealth, although we must use it differently and can share it only conditionally—within the terms of our individual isolation. We are separate, and each is special, but we are not alien to each other.

Let me summarize these facts, each of which is objectively verifiable, consistently true. Each of us is delimited by the surface of our skin, and is drastically different, inside that surface, from what lies outside. Our continued existence consists of transfers of energy between our insides and the external universe, and these transfers involve, for the most part, drastic changes of state. In fact, if these differences and changes were not maintained, we would be dead. In particular, that part of our insides most closely allied with our thoughts, perceptions, feelings, and actions—our nervous system—is structured in a way to force all the internal-exter-

nal transfers with which it is directly involved through a surface shell of minute, distinct, disjunct impulses. The only
connections of sense, perception, understanding, and coordi-
nated, purposeful action occur within us, within this shell.
About what remains outside we are forced forever to guess.
If we turn to each other—perhaps in an attempt to mollify
our isolation by finding similarities between us—we are met
by an objective paradox: our sensations, the precision of
which we can share because our sensory equipment is stan-
dard, cannot stand still long enough to share; within our
sensory-motor shells, where we make connections and seek
stability, we find that we vary the most from each other. Particular correlation is beyond consideration. Finally, each of
us is isolated from any larger social and/or natural systems,
as we understand them and make them orderly, purposive,
and predictable, by the wealth of our internal potential, and
the consequent unpredictability of our internal states.

Although they are objectively verifiable, it is consistent
with these facts to observe that in our interpretation of
them, in our search for their meaning, and in our attempts
to apply them to our actions, you and I will differ greatly.
The facts themselves are simple. What we make of them and
how we use them are far from simple matters: they are as
complicated as we ourselves are. Yet I am compelled to make
four suggestions about them which will begin to let you
know how I interpret them. First, our personal failures and
our social crimes against the individual are all associated
with insufficient observation of the constant, objective truth
of these facts, and our inconsistent application of them to
our behavior. Second, our primary motive in ignoring them
is *fear:* we are afraid to face them, and this leads to fear of
ourselves and fear of each other. Third, if we *do* accept their
truth and attempt to live with them consistently, we commit
ourselves to a great deal of hard work, as well as to the necessity of enduring a great deal of uncertainty, even despair.

Fourth, despite this risk, our greatest pleasures, our capacities for communication, and our integrated life come through our whole acceptance of their truth.

You may not be impressed with the facts that I have mustered here on these pages before you read them, the ones that demonstrate your isolation from all else, including me and what you see of me. But listen, contrary to many sober opinions, you are crazy if you assume that your understanding of the world and the world itself are close companions. In fact, they are often enemies. Since your survival depends on maintaining certain essential transactions with the world that lies outside you, this fact seems important to know.

Perhaps you don't believe me. Perhaps the environment in which you have grown up has shown few, if any, threats, and has seemed full of support and kindness. But it is important to realize that the conditions which prevail, for example, in an affluent American suburb are extremely rare. In most places on earth, over most periods of time, the environmental pressures on human beings have been—and still are—relentless and unforgiving. Time after time, disaster after disaster has shown that although our natural environment provides our wherewithal, it has no particular interest in our survival. Nature's eye, when it surveys its domain, is disinterested and impersonal. Survival for any species has always been a struggle. I do not mean by this to suggest a nature "red in tooth and claw" so much as the much grimmer thought that if we choose to kill ourselves off, nothing out there will try to stop us.

Since most instances of disaster have so far been outlived by some who remained to record and interpret them, we at least know that disaster is possible. Beyond that we must recognize how our perceptions have been sheltered from the disastrous truth. Not simply is our knowledge of these events filtered through the recording process itself—often at tremendous remove from the facts, and always different from the experience—and not only is the chronicler biased, at the least, by his particular sense of whom he is speaking to, and unavoidably, at the most, by the fact that he is alive while those who really know what a disaster is are (by definition) dead, whereas he can speak only of of his life and toward some living purpose—but beyond these distortions is the ultimate distortion that the rest of us, those to whom the chronicler speaks, are also alive and caught up in our living: we can perceive a disaster only from the vantage point of life. And even if, from time to time, we notice to ourselves that the dead were once alive or that we may at some time be dead, their real and our imagined agony, whatever its form, is always softly cushioned on our present, continuing survival.

There is a special arrogance associated with survival, an arrogance which, via ideas like "the survival of the fittest," comes to characterize apologists or enthusiasts for the existing structure of society or condition of the species, taken as a whole. This arrogance, which might be called the arrogance of comfort, or more basically the arrogance of the survivor, rests on a set of assumptions which include a faith in the endlessness of human opportunity, in the ultimate chance of reconciliation between man's hopes for himself and the actual conditions of his survival, and in the obvious, unquestionable assertion—so far, at least—that any particular person or group of people has always died but "the species" has "always" survived. By "the species" is meant, of course, all the survivors. Nothing succeeds like success: nothing survives like survivors. Those who are now dead may once have been living members of the species, may once have been normal, but now that they are dead they are critically abnormal.

Not just outmoded, but suspect. Even subversive.

The gentle message of the dead that we are mortal picks away at the arrogance of the living. Each of us will some time be struck down, they whisper. But if each of us is mortal then all of us are mortal, and if all of us are mortal then it is possible that we could all die at once, at which time not only would our arrogance be tempered, but there would be no survivors. Our mortality is indeed a subversive message if carried to this length, yet it is only wishful thinking that would call this conclusion unreasonable or impossible.

A broad tradition contrasts individual mortality with the "immortality" of the species, and within this tradition, compared to the species, the ordinary individual lacks virtue, dignity, or even much significance. In this tradition, death is but the final indignity, the ultimate proof, to each of us, of his sinfulness. But if we recognize the possible mortality of the species perhaps this tradition will be overturned. Perhaps the dead, although subversive in their silent way, are not sinful. Perhaps in some ways each dead man has as much dignity as the entire living species. May I confess that some of my best friends are dead?

Recently, in new ways, we have been forced to question our faith in the survival of the species, dignified or not. There are intelligent, knowledgeable men who give the ant better odds than the human race. Indeed, there are intelligible perspectives from which we can see the human race as a galactic virus, a small, cancerous infection of the universe, clearly parasitic—not yet, and perhaps never, symbiotic. Although in the past it has seemed a truism to say that our strength lies in our numbers, the suspicion is gaining substance that our ultimate weakness may also lie in our numbers: that it may be our species as a whole which will manage (in its unmanageability) to kill us all. So once again it is necessary to question the comfortable arrogance of our survival so far, its apologists and its enthusiasts. That is, we must face the facts that human opportunity is not endless, that the species may not live forever—or even for a long time—and that therefore we cannot always expect to be comfortable: our hopes will always remain alienated from the environmental conditions of our survival. Under such circumstances of discomfort, danger, and essential loneliness, the individual has as much dignity as the species. Perhaps more.

If this is so, it seems reasonable to suspect that the various experiences of individual alienation, from the broadest to the most intimate, may be examples of the realization that the species will *not* take care of itself, that those who are comfortable are *not* to be trusted, and that a predisposed suspicion, applied equally to ourselves and to others— especially as we are socially organized—is an intelligent adaptation.

As it is ordinarily used, alienation refers to a state of our having lost our trust subsequent to a state in which we still trusted, when we did not feel isolated, and when the experience of trust was trustworthy. We imply, by contrasting these states, that somehow the facts of our isolation which I stated in the previous section did not at that prior time pertain or even, by some warp of the physical universe, were not true. By this view, we work from a contrast between the health of infant unity to the unhealth of adult alienation. The alienated person, in our comfortable society, is "sick," or at least so say those who are most comfortable—those, that is, who are most simply supported by the incredible complexities of our society. To grow up, these comfortable people say, is to retain as many of the conditions of childhood as possible, yet the unhappy person, the alienated person, is in some way being "immature." Is not the simpler surmise that this oblique reference to the unity of the infant experience is a reference to an illusion of unity, to a feeling of unity, to a perception of unity, even to a convincing experience of unity, but not, it turns out, to an actual state of unity? And that our conditioned trust in the continuing benevolence of our environment is based on special, highly expensive, local conditions—parochial and precarious?

If we feel that our alienation is a fall from the grace of an innocent, trusting infancy, when through our eyes even this world was an Eden, we blame the world for our disillusionment—as if the world had any less desire integrally to be itself than we! But suppose that what we call alienation, wiped clean of negative connotation and nostalgia, is a symptom of our learning, an act of adaptation, a motion toward survival, a recognition of the real which, if we believe many of the literary, religious, psychosocial, medical, and historical efforts of the last two hundred years, is a better hypothesis than its naive opposite?

There is much that suggests that we are matter first, and that thought—even the most congenial—is only secondary and in some ways foreign to our nature. It is easy to imagine that you are, first (and last), a thing. How else explain your mortality? All you have to do is imagine being on a battlefield—there are numerous examples to pick from—about to be converted into a lump of burned and broken flesh, and you cannot help asking, with intelligent suspicion, whether the words that anybody chants to justify your predicament, the songs that marched your feet in that direction, the threats of punishment that limited your alternatives, even your own proud thought which may have brought you there, are anything more than temptations in a deadly con game. Were you really given life in order to be *deluded* into death? If I choose to die for my country, at least spare me the lies! Because I belong to it, my flesh, at least, is my own.

We may, as Erikson says, have to learn to be ready to die. We also have to learn to be ready to live, and one lesson is that of freedom. Freedom goes in many guises, and we seek it in different ways. One kind of freedom is granted us at

birth: an innocent opportunity which each must defend
against the encroachments of a manipulative world. But as
we grow, other kinds of opportunity become threatened, and
unavoidably some of these threats become internalized so
that we carry them around inside us. I refer not just to ugly
memories or childhood trauma, but also to long-forgotten
habits of thought which, by their innocent assumptions
about what is true, or what is good, or what kind of person
we can or cannot trust, leave us blinded. To free ourselves
from internal blindness we may have to learn to distrust ourselves in painful ways, ways that destroy certain kinds of happiness forever. These acts of learning are also acts of alienation. Right there, again and anew, the *issue* of freedom
revives: what do we buy with this loss of happiness? Doubt,
including self-doubt, does present us with choices not otherwise open. In those moments of freedom it takes an effort to
see the alternatives clearly. One direction is clear, toward cynicism: an initial act of debunking becomes habit, and the
habit is easily reinforced simply because doubt always leads
to further discovery. The cynic is one to whom this discovery
remains a pleasant disappointment, a disappointment which
he shares in triumphant gloom. Or, more gently, he may re-
tire into a life of constant suspicion, of wavering and hesitation, which he shares by "always thinking otherwise," his
weapon the pinprick, his accomplishment the deflated intention.

The cynic can only be successful, but his victory is cheap:
he wins by neglect. Whether it is the shock of the initial experience of successful doubt, or self-congratulation at the initial experience of insight, for some reason the cynic stops
short, and the issue remains to him that of doubt versus belief. What he neglects to acknowledge is the simple, experiential fact that once you begin to doubt, you cannot stop.
There is no reason to stop. Doubting is an act no longer of
choice but of rational compulsion. What is left to choose

about is, what to do then? In other words, doubt leads first to a *question*, a real question. A real question is not just a thought, or a collection of words or symbols somewhere, or some form of logical structure. A real question is a state of your being, a total state, in which there is suddenly created a large space between thought and action, an empty space across which there are no roads, no tracks, no signposts, no evidence of habitation; you do not know how to start across, what will happen on the other side—if there is one—or why you should undertake the journey. Much less do you know whether you will be happy along the way, or when you get there. Even the simplest actions are suddenly difficult, and confident decisions distant. What once took no time now takes only time, and your doubt only increases the delay.

Let the cynic, in his haste to debunk, turn his doubt on his own doubting, and if he is honest he must come to something else: he must start walking into that real space of question. This alternative to cynicism is just as real.

In a confrontation between the naive belief that the truth can be caught and held firm, and a consistent doubt, doubt must win. But if, instead of stopping there we ask further, the choice is whether to be satisfied with doubt alone or to entertain the suspicion that doubt works because the truth is somewhere else, alive and kicking; in other words, that doubt is as much an instrument of life as it is of deadness. Our doubt insists that we cannot be sure of this possibility —it must remain only an intimation of joy—just as it insists on the transiency of gloom. In this state of indeterminancy we can, at last, begin to experience some of the more powerful emotions of our humanity: compassion, for example, and clean curiosity. And in rare moments of balance, we can even cross a century to feel love or irony. These moments convince us for all time that, no matter what happens, we are human and know what it is to be human. Of these moments even doubt cannot deprive us because it has al-

ready brought us here, and only lifts our experience beyond
understanding.

That is the first thing I would like to say about recognizing our isolation, our aloneness, our alienation: that via
doubt it leaves us with *double vision*. Not only are we forced
to realize that things are seldom what they seem, but that
any act of understanding is an incomplete effort of composi-
tion: that understanding involves bringing together what
seems with something else—a something else which always
must remain in question, hidden in the desert of doubt.
Where that desert is, whether it is within us or outside us,
we do not and cannot know. So for the time being (which is
all the time we have) we must assume it is in both places.
Facing the knowledge of my subjectivity, I have faith: my
guessing about truth is, I suppose, part of the truth, yet as I
guess, I must stand aside from reality. My guessing is part of
the truth and isn't, at the same time.

As it defines a special kind of mental experience, double
vision will be a recurring theme here. The term has a medical meaning first, describing the condition of a person's
being unable to synthesize the visual fields of his two eyes
into a single image. I do not intend pathological connota-
tions when I use the term, but I do mean an uneasiness in
the experience. Double vision always forces us to look farther, to move ahead. Specifically, the ingredients of the experience are two distinct, present fields of sensation, each or-
dered within itself but sharing no common order with the
other—each connected to the other only by the vehicle of
our awareness of the two at the same time. Our relationship
to them is limited to our awareness: we are held back from
understanding them in a single way, or by extrapolation
from describing an explanation of their relationship (even in
silence to ourselves) which is based on a single, uncontradic-
tory set of assumptions. I will from time to time use this experience as an analogy applied to mental "fields"—organized

areas of thought—rather than to visual fields of other kinds of sensation. We experience an example of this mental doubleness when, after the passage of time, we return to a situation which we once understood in one way and now understand differently because of changes in ourselves. If our memory is clear and our two understandings—past and present—are whole, we can experience their simultaneous truth, even though they are in clear conflict and suggest contradictory behavior.

The dynamics of double vision define the most interesting characteristics of our life, and predetermine—if endless grappling can be predetermined—our perceptions, upon which we base every single act of survival. Despite the implied urgency of this last observation, in a more relaxed frame of mind one can see that it is our isolation which makes the problems of understanding, of communication, of disillusionment, of commitment, and of love interesting rather than trivial. Learning to live is not simply a matter of adding experience on experience, but of undergoing thorough changes in our perceptions of the world and of ourselves.

The second thing I would like to say about alienation is that if we recognize it, we must also recognize that it has strong implications about our perceptual priorities. In fact, what comes first to us when we open our senses to the world around us is *the total field of our sensations*. In our isolation, sensation is all that is given us, but its totality is enormous—much larger and more complicated than, at any moment or over any period of time, we can appreciate. Our sensory field is not normally deprived, but our inhibitions and habits limit our perceptions. In this I do not only mean that we select what we shall respond to. Of course we must. If we didn't select, we would—under the conditions of our physiology—entertain chaos. No, what I mean is that we tend not to vary in our selectivity, and rather than select one set of stimuli now and another totally different set later, we stick with the more familiar. This, too, is natural: the habitual and familiar are not only conservative, they are also friendly. So again we find that freedom—at least the freedom of openness to the new—is not easy, and involves an effort, indeed a peculiar kind of effort. Trying to open oneself to the totality of sensation at any given time is a motion away from compression, from direction, from choice, from coherence, and, as such, an effort away from effort. Openness is difficult, yet it is the only way we can begin to use our most natural resource, the full advantage of sensation. One who deprives us of sensation murders us, whether or not we continue to breathe.

In this respect I am my own worst enemy: not only, in clinging to an evenness of experience, do I restrict and govern what I will notice—a loss between me and my environment—but I also treat you (and anyone else) as if, at this moment, what I say were the most important part of your sensory input. I assume your attention. In some humility, let me admit that although I may be laboring over this manuscript, the result can be only a small part of your total environment. There is nothing I can or would do to change that.

Do not ignore the resource of your total environment. Within it all experience starts with equal rights, and the totality must be allowed to assert its own order. Compared to it, no single person can be more than a small part of it and must always stand the test: "Which makes more sense, what this person says (and what I guess he means), or all my experience of the world?" I hope you are convinced of your right to make such a test: *it is guaranteed by your isolation.* In addition, remembering that it is difficult to remain open to your environment, be aware how easy it is to be distracted from it, blackmailed into ignoring it, or simply deprived of it. It is rare that you would be locked up in total isolation from sensation, but it is common indeed that you will be: (1) persuaded to ignore obvious facts by social pressure; (2) trapped into undesirable commitments by calculated rewards; (3) deluded by suggestive propaganda or even a neighbor's back-fence rhetoric; (4) misled into addicted behavior, where the ruts of habit are so deep they form virtual blinders; (5) enticed to surrender your autonomy, before you have even possessed it, by dreams of an intimacy able to cure the pains and perils of loneliness; (6) beguiled by "reason" into believing, contrary to fact, that certain kinds of thought and areas of consideration are invulnerable to disruption or contradiction by even small penetrations of new experience; or (7) caught up in a frenzy of antireason and persuaded, by your emotional identification with a certain mood or movement, that you have transcended your boundaries, and that you are somehow more important to all other people than each of them is to you. The world is full of con men, conscious and unconscious, and they all know that deception is largely a matter of letting you do what you want to do— which is to ignore all the information in your environment which would reveal the effort that your autonomy and freedom constantly require.

The shoe fits your foot, too. Surely it has been your pleasure (reinforced by success) to deceive others by playing on their laziness in this way. It may seem strange, but I would rather see you deceive consciously than in ignorance. But most of all I would rather you did not deceive, and that you knew you didn't. Very difficult! Meanwhile, just as the context of your own freedom and the largeness of your real environment is your personal protection against anyone's deceit, so is his environment his protection against your deceit. You cannot claim his entire attention, nor do you have a right to. Besides, he will not give it to you, and you would be foolish to expect it. It is inconsistent to claim your own freedom without granting theirs to others. Unless you are a crook or simply lazy. "Whatever progress may be taken to mean, it can't mean making the world any easier a place to save your soul . . . your decency, your integrity." [2]

Well, there's my essay on alienation. Its brevity is explained by our overexposure to both the word and the idea. Yet I am convinced that we can't begin to accept or understand the last century or two's history without double vision, nor act without basing our integrity on our total experience. How else can we accommodate our knowledge of the unforgivable crimes which have been, and continue to be, committed on good people, and on the other hand, a confidence that in some subterranean way, truth and survival go hand in hand? How else can we unify understanding achieved by argument with understanding achieved by experience and example? It is only as we are educated by doubt that we have a chance of finding anything at all in which to have faith. And it is only by straining to recognize and react to our total environment that each of us has a reliable basis of either doubt or faith. Contrary to both optimistic and pessimistic notions of human history, and with no implications of progress (despite the fact that one can hardly mention the word survival without some Darwinian echo), with the last century's sophistication we have not necessarily gained anything of pleasure or delight, nor have we fallen from grace. No, it is just that the terms in which we see ourselves, and consequently the terms in which we understand the idea of our survival, have undeniably and unavoidably changed.

MOST people who drive by the place have no reason to notice it. In your typical automobile scenery, it's

[2] Robert Frost, quoted in Lawrance Thompson, *Robert Frost: The Years of Triumph* (New York: Holt, Rinehart and Winston Inc., First Edition, 1970), p. 387, from "Robert Frost on Sixtieth Birthday Talks of Joys of Living," *Amherst Student*, March 25, 1935.

an unplace: a shallow, heavily wooded gully running up a
steep, heavily wooded hillside which starts right at the road-
side, so you would have to lean down to look up it out the
window. Nor can you see it before or after you pass: it is hidden in a curve of the road, which dips just there, too. It is
perfect for an ambush, but of course it is my wartime experience which makes me say that. My experience as a guerrilla,
I mean. Hiding up the slope of that very hillside, living, for
the length of the game, in a cave.

Once a summer, during the years when the Real World
was a busy killing-machine, with my wooden-barreled Gar-
and in hand and on my head a fiber-plastic helmet liner
bought after much begging at the surplus store (I still cannot fathom the incongruency of midwar surplus), I struggled
up that hillside in the pine and maple shade, avoiding the
patches of sun not just because they were hot but because I
was already beginning to hide. About two hundred feet up
the slope I reached a collection of boulders from behind
which I could point my rifle and squeeze the trigger when a
car passed. A few feet higher a huge slab of granite (it is in
New Hampshire) leaned on another, leaving a space below
which I called a cave. At the rear of the cave a narrow passage crawled back up to daylight, large enough to be an escape tunnel, although more often it became a chimney dis-
persing imaginary smoke. Because, you see, while I was
there, with my invisible, invented band of companions, I
lived there all year—cooking, sleeping, being miserable in
bad weather while we waited for the enemy to come along
the road below. They would never find us here although,
without doubt, they would come looking. That is what hills
are for: for partisans to hide in, and for the enemy, with his
machines and machine guns, to search.

Simply by waiting in silence we always won. We were
never found. In half an hour or so the game was over, and I
would descend again, sliding on the slippery maple leaves
and pine needles, scrambling down through the weeds and

over hot bare rock patches, and finally leap off the bank onto the road in the last spasm of attack. The asphalt jolted my teeth and left my feet numb.

By accident of age, the only violence I knew was imagined like this—dark fantasies peopled with wartime comic-book caricatures or an occasional highlighted picture from a movie: a man desperately firing a submachine gun at an unseen enemy surrounding him in the mist as the final credits started dribbling up the screen. Or Ingrid Bergman watching Gary Cooper being left behind to delay the Spanish Fascists at the pass, at the price of his life. You could wish she cared about you half as much! The accoutrements of violence were much more important than violence, just as a live hero is more important to the public than any dead man, hero or not. That puts violence at one remove. And if you realize that I hardly saw the accoutrements—a few flashcards of airplane silhouettes—you can begin to see why violence, for me, has remained only imaginary. War can only be fantastic, its addicts insane.

Only on two occasions did all that fantasy touch anything real. The first time was when a neighbor cut down the enormous elm that stood on our common property line, and it fell into the alder swamp behind our house, through which a friend and I, every afternoon for a week the previous summer, had chased and fled from the Japanese. In the process of our cleaning up the fallen tree, the sun came through where the alders had stood, and the jungle with its tunneled paths disappeared into dry light. The other occasion occurred when our sixth-grade class walked to see a display of military equipment laid out on a lawn on the other side of town. Filled with excited thoughts that these empty ammunition boxes might be refilled, and that this half-track might return to battle, I joined the children who had started scribbling their names in chalk on a large rubber raft which floated, orange and official, on the grass. When it was reinflated beside a downed plane in the middle of the ocean, our names would unfold with it and pop into that new world! The next day my teacher kept me after school and, her usually pleasant face pink with erratic anger, bawled me out —apparently for trying to connect myself, via my chalked name, to the actual war. My action had been disorderly, improper, perhaps presumptuous.

In the face of this more homely and less harmful violence, my fantasy was driven deeper into dreams and became gentled. If the real war, on the other side of the world, wanted my real participation, it would have to come find me. Meanwhile, I would walk down the road and climb up this hill, so that when it came looking, parading down the road below, I would see it first—and hold my tongue as it walked past, and watch all those uniformed legs keeping step, those leveled eyes unaware of my gaze from above.

Oh, I know what it is to march, too. Later, I put on the uniform and marched with the high school band. We weren't fancy. We did no patterned prancing at football games. The main event, for us, was marching, come spring, in the Memorial Day parade, up Front Street, through the cemetery, and back down Main Street to the town hall. Our part was small, but I remember clearly—and in the right mood the memory can squeeze tears into my eyes—the band of ancient, white-haired men in stiff-collared purple and blue uniforms, carrying pale brass cornets and a battered sousaphone, who out of some year-long hiding place came to march at the head of the procession, leading us limpingly along the long trek. When the graveyard was reached, while everyone else was silent, it was they who knew the proper, slow pace by which to play Chopin's funeral march to the central ceremony, and after the memorial volley, with muffled drums to walk us out again: awkward, corny, and intensely sad. In those days, even after two world wars, we were still mourning the Civil War, a piece of carnage which puts patriotism in a peculiar light, and tends to purify sadness.

Well, from my hillside vantage, I will let those old men pass. But all you others had better watch out—you in your uniforms of service or signals of office who expect my obeisance rather than to share a human sadness. Nor you others who mob along the street breaking windows with angry voice or rocks (it doesn't matter which): you cannot make me share your madness or your badness just by insisting. Whatever parade you march in, you must finally come to the hills and disperse to find what you are looking for. I will wait for you here, and if you wish to join me, I will let you pass. Otherwise, expect a few surprises. My rifle may be wooden and my helmet thin plastic, but I am not frightened. The boulders are large and loose here, and I start higher on the hill.

4 You and Me

Each of us exists separately, and the basic terms of our isolation are clear, close to absolute. In a broader way, our isolation is attested to by the very large numbers of other people in the world with whom each of us has had no relationship at all—we never meet them, have no concrete sense of who they are, nor how they are specifically different from us. Even among the people we do meet, our dealings with most are brief, transitory contacts as we slide by each other: ricochets rather than relationships.

Yet there are some few people for each of us with whom we involve ourselves deeply. We may bounce off them, but we return again and again. We come to care for them, to respond to their presence with attention, and to shape our decisions differently because they exist. Members of the family, friends with whom we share new experiences, older people whose life-styles we respect and who give us—effortlessly—a

sense of our own worth and capacity to be valuable people,
younger people whom we like and who seem to like us: these
people have faces and feelings, and we expect to share our
selves with them. The difference in how we feel toward
these people and all the rest of "people" is enormous, and
this contrast focuses our emotions, channels our most urgent
efforts, and at times—if we work at it and are lucky—
invokes a strong sense in us that we can transcend our personal, individual isolation. Confrontation leads to connection, which leads to communication.

Our transcendent sense of communication with another
person exists. And because it seems to deny, to contradict,
the facts of our isolation, it raises some serious questions.
The more forceful our experience of communication, the
stronger the questions become. As our sense of connection
with another individual comes and goes, can we trust it, or is
it an illusion, a form of delusion—a kind of mutual, mental
backrub? Conversely, if it is a form of truth, does our experience of it justify ignoring our factual isolation? Is communication "more important than" isolation? Should we seek it as
our most esteemed goal and in so doing should we suppress
or drastically modify our equally strong experiences of isolation? Can we plan our lives and choose our circumstances in
such a way that our sense of communication with others becomes a more-or-less permanent state? Can we share this
sense of communication with more people than those we
meet face-to-face and familiarly? What is the relationship between communication and community? If this sense of communication is a form of truth, and as we experience it, more
delightful and important to us than any other activity, why
do we bother to do anything else with our time but seek it?
Why do we ask others to do anything else? How can we
avoid the obstacles, the practical problems which seem to
cause endless partings, even from those closest to us? Can we
be sure that our pleasures in communication and our con-

stant desire for their delights are not in fact destructive—
self-indulgent weaknesses which, if we give in to them, will
leave us open to betrayal and intimate pain? Can communication kill?

I cannot answer these questions. I do not believe that they
have any firm, fixed answers. But that is no reason not to
think about them, nor is it impossible to say anything definite at all. We *can* make some statements about our communication with each other that are consistent both with our
factual isolation and with our communicative experiences. I will make four such statements, but before I do, I
would, if I could, invent and use a mental eraser to obliter-
ate from your mind and memory the following metaphors
and their implications:

> Communication involves sending and receiving mes-
>   sages.
> Understanding is a process of decoding messages.
> Different media are merely different codes.
> Communication is a way of getting something done.
> Communication is a matter of saying what you think
>   and of understanding what others way.
> Language is a cipher. Scientific language enciphers
>   the reality of the world; artistic language enci-
>   phers the reality of the self. Therefore, science is
>   truth-expression, art is self-expression.
> The basic divisions of the human experience are be-
>   tween "objective" and "subjective" reality, or be-
>   tween "conceptual" and "affective" perception:
>   therefore, these are the basic divisions of human
>   communication.
> Learning is essentially a process of internalizing and
>   using new languages, new ciphers, new codes: a
>   business code, a banking code, a legal code, a psy-
>   chological code, a physics code, an architectural de-

sign code, etc., etc.

Good communication is necessary for good business, good education, good banking, good human relations, good feelings, good living, good whatever, etc.

It's not that these statements have nothing at all to do with reality. It's just that I wish, while I discuss the meaning of the four statements I will make, that these others didn't exist. Their existence is bound to interfere. They are like a swarm of black flies. They land on you and, in an incredible parody of purpose, hunch their shoulders and start to burrow around. So great is their eagerness to bite that they cannot stand still long enough to sink their teeth. They tingle the alarms of your skin but do not attempt to fly away when you swat them. Their nuisance is in their numbers and their nerve. Nothing is more pathetic than the attack of one black fly; nothing more disastrous than a swarm of them, which can turn a peaceful spot in the wilderness into a hell one can only wish to leave at a dead run.

Just find a spot that is temporarily free of those statements I mentioned, if you can, while I try to expose some of the contents of my own four statements. But before I make each statement, let me catch my breath in the clear air of experience:

IN the blank, impersonal wall of forgetfulness that separates me from that summer seventeen years ago there are several blurred-edge holes through which I glimpse clearly some moments, some scenes which would take pages of explanation to connect: how the five of us got there, why we went, what we were doing, and what our relationship was, most of which I could dredge up, all right, but I don't want to get sidetracked. It's enough to say that we were there, on Chena Ridge outside Fairbanks, Alaska, messily encamped on Charlie's sister's homestead, and that the sun didn't go down for the six weeks we were there—a time so gloriously strange, so dislocated, so alien that instead of being unreal it was intensely actual: no distractions from the society which Americans call the "real world" but which is really only a mass hallucination, the largest-selling drug on the market. I want to tell you about Nick and Pete.

I stopped briefly at the top of the pipeline that first day of work, standing on the three-foot, rusted steel pipe that supplied the entire mining operation, feeling it tremble slightly as the water within rushed down the hillside and hit bottom where the pipe bent horizontal just as it crossed a river and then branched and rebranched across the mile-wide, flat-gravel-bottomed crater which had once been a narrow, soft-soiled valley. Against the far earth cliff, now and then I caught a glimpse of the low, flat arc of white water which melted the permafrost and washed away the powdery soil down to the gravel. The heavily muddied water found its way to the river, which flowed eastward, depositing whole hillsides of sludge who knows where. To the west, beyond some trees, I could see the dredge, which by some unnatural magic made and moved the lake in which it floated, scooping down into the gravel, scrabbling sometimes fifty feet to bedrock, where for centuries the prize had sifted, bringing up the whole slushy mixture bucket by bucket and flushing it through a sluiceway, where the heavier precious metals were trapped, and spewing the valueless remainder out behind. The trailings, loosened from centuries of compaction, towered over the dredge; where it traveled it raised the valley floor a good twenty-five feet, molded into a great gravel corduroy pattern, unwalkable, unbeautiful, useless. Moonsville.

I met the young foreman, Gerard, at his car which was parked in a clearing at the foot of the main pipe. He was sitting, foot up on a log, chewing gum. "You Lloyd?" he said, and I said, "Yes," and sat down on a rock. Pretty soon, slamming into the morning's stillness, drove a plywood-sided pick-up, which swung around and stopped. Two young Eskimos jumped out the back and were followed by an older man, who climbed laboriously down. The right-hand door swung open, and a young red-bearded guy in a red, lettered baseball cap got out and walked over to greet the foreman. As the truck drove away, the other three didn't say anything, but the foreman and his pal talked softly, lazily, until Gerard glanced at his watch. "It's seven-thirty. Let's go," he said, standing up suddenly. "Bring the stuff." He waved at a pile of tools beside the log and stalked off east on the trail. I picked up a shovel and a crow bar and followed redbeard, who was already close behind the foreman.

I was in that superwatchful, supercareful state in which you approach a new job, when you are particularly susceptible to formalities, not out of fear of making a fool of yourself, but looking for the patterns—of work, of pace, of conversation—so that you can assume them, assimilate them, forget them. As the six of us filed singly through that surreal, seventy-year-old landscape, I was trying to anticipate what we would be doing, looking for clues in every detail I could see. We passed a solitary nozzle-man, fifty yards away, carving at the bank with his wet, cold torch. He stood barely moving, his slicker dripping from the backmist, intent on his slow, violent work. He didn't notice us.

As I rounded a mound of gravel I heard a click, and some pebbles near the top made a brief, miniature landslide. I looked up and then behind to see if the others had seen what had caused it. The two Eskimos were about twenty feet back, their faces expressionless as they shouldered their heavy loads of tools along the trail. Fifty feet behind them the old man, shovel dangling at armlength, keep his eyes on the ground as he picked his way slowly. Nothing, I guess.

Those stones waited until that moment, and I just happened to be there. Or maybe a chipmunk. I sloshed through a shallow pool that lay across the trail, and something plocked into the water four feet to my right, sending up a tiny geyser. I had bombarded enough model boats in my childhood to know that it was a lump of dirt: nothing else gives such a perfect miniature imitation of naval artillery. I looked around again, expecting some sign, but no, the same scene. The two Eskimos walking impassively behind me, only the old man was further back. I turned back and thought, as I walked, had it really happened? Yes. What did it mean? Who had done it? Why? Just then a pebble landing in the mud, again four feet to my right, and without stopping, thinking, or looking, I scooped up a small clod of mud and tossed it back over my head. What came out of nowhere must be returned to nowhere. I heard it hit water and glanced around. Both Eskimos were smiling, with a special ease. We didn't stop walking, nor did we speak, but our non-aggressive bombardment continued until we caught up with redbeard and the foreman, where they waited. "O.K., here's where we start," said Gerard.

That was how it lined up for the summer. Gerard told us what to do and sat around watching; the only emotion I saw him express was irritation when his clothes were accidentally dirtied. Redbeard picked the cleanest part of the work and did as little as he could, using his conversation with Gerard as a time-killer. Adolf (the old man) did just enough to keep from being fired, shrunken into a jittery defensiveness of unknown origin. So, while Gerard and redbeard chatted about college and fraternities and career plans and girls, and Adolf occasionally muttered to himself but never spoke, Nick, Pete, and I did most of the work, which consisted of laying and shifting the pipe and moving the nozzles which had washed themselves out of work. The three of us had tremendous fun together without thinking, in the exhilaration of common exertion, uncomplicated competition, laughing at each other's mistakes, playing small tricks on each other, telling make-believe lies and delighting in being found out, but never prying. Even the misery of a rainy day became an important part of our communication: the funniest joke of all was when one of us slipped and fell in the mud—the wetter he got the funnier. We didn't need to talk much (they spoke pretty good English, and taught me some Eskimo, all of which I have now forgotten, except "airplane"—*tingmashook*—and "big airplane"—*tingmashook tik pluk*) —and knew what to do without being told (which made Gerard uneasy because he felt he had to tell us anyway—it was his job after all), and within our easy teamwork we became masters of the one-word, one-gesture joke. The work was hard enough, but the day passed quickly between laughing, and I didn't notice any fatigue until the end of each day, when I had to leave them and walk the mile and a half up the pipeline and along the road to our camp for supper with the others, while Nick and Pete caught the truck back to the company camp, where they would live until work ended in the fall and they went home with some money. Five weeks passed rapidly.

I had spoken so much about Nick and Pete to the others that it was suggested that I ask them to come for supper some night, so on the next to last day of work for me I asked them to supper the next day, and they shrugged and smiled and said, "Sure." The following day, when four-thirty came, we started walking back from the last nozzle I would ever move, not saying much. When we came to the bottom of the main line where it crossed the river, I started toward it, and they stopped on the road and looked at me. And I stopped and turned and, in complete surprise, said, "Aren't you coming?" and they looked at each other, and Pete shook his head quickly once, and Nick said, "We've got to get back to the camp," and they both looked relieved when I said, "O.K."

So I went over and shook hands and said, "Good-bye," and they smiled and turned and started off down the road.

All the way up the pipeline I wondered why they had changed their minds. I still don't know. Maybe they didn't like the idea of a sad ceremony that anticipated nothing. Maybe they suspected me of anthropology.

1 **In our relationships with those we closely and constantly confront, reconfront, and come to know and care about, we are forced to recognize and come to terms with our mutual independence.**

You recognize this independence in two important ways, two ways in which you see the other person as real: first, as he is different from you, both immediately and in the long run; and second, as in your mind he is free of any systematic social constraints. In other words, your expectations toward the other are not preconditioned—neither by your private wish for undisturbed equilibrium, nor by preconceptions of how your friend fits into any social system—family, school, job, political or social ideology. If your mutual expectations are free in these two ways as your relationship develops, then it can amplify, and is defended against extraneous intrusions.

If you seek, within your relationship, specific constancy from the other—to your mood, to your need for tolerance and reinforcement—or a feeling of mutual usefulness, perceptual agreement, or even simple presence, you will not find it. Between any two people at any given time the congruence of their internal states or the smoothness of their interaction are largely matters of good luck and habit, slightly laced with attention often focused not on the other person but on a job to be done, some mutual involvement in an activity lying outside both. Such involvement can make differences—inevitable between people—constructive in a nonthreatening way. In any case, whether the mutual involvement is direct (pointed at each other) or indirect (pointed at a common task), interpersonal differences are food for mutual growth. Separateness and independence are essential ingredients of the reality of a relationship, and the value of the relationship to you lies in its power to enhance your individual reality—your own total reality as you are, rather than just your consciousness of reality, which must always be partial.

Your view of another (and his of you) is continually modified not only by direct, mutually conscious communication, but also by the fact that you can see him in situations where his attention is on something other than you: you can see him from the "blind side" of his consciousness. You come to know him in ways he cannot know himself, and vice versa. This "unexpected" knowledge can be a source of friction (e.g. when you are surprised by his disapproval, by his outwitting you, or by his sudden, unwelcome descriptions of your behavior), but it is also a source of great trust. Because you know him in ways he cannot know himself, the gift of your love is enormously amplified—and his in return—well beyond the understanding of either.

The *internal* threats to relationship are many and find unique form at any instant, but in general they can be described as overactive, delusionary attempts toward mutual identity. Such attempts create extreme possibilities: stifling, short-range euphoria—the bliss of apparent "total" understanding—and in inevitable reaction, acute frustration and fierce cruelty. It is a rare pair who can sustain their reality through such extremes, which define a dialectic of destruction, not love.

The *external* threats to relationship are less acutely emotional and more clearly perceptual. If, as you look at the other person, you see him as part of a social system, you in-

troduce an extraneous demand: that he be representative of
that system. In so doing, you diminish his reality for you in
two main ways. First, you tend to filter out those aspects of
his actual behavior which contradict your assumptions—you
pay less attention to him and more to your idea of him. Second, when his contradictory behavior does manage to pene-
trate your screen of conscious expectation, your reaction is
more likely to be a feeling of betrayal. In not playing the social role you have assigned to him, he has let you down. In
fact, it is you who have betrayed him by expecting him to be
something he is not and cannot be: an idea in your head.

I doubt that there is a person in the world who has not
been subjected to this exquisite and most painful form of
torture: the energetic (sometimes unconscious) nagging by a
person close to you that you conform to that person's idea of
what you should be, accompanied by the frustrating sense
that he is so blinded by his idea that he cannot begin to see
you. Even the distant disapproval of a mild acquaintance can
put you on the rack. Sometimes you react in more extreme
opposition just to become visible, and suddenly you are ac-
cused of total betrayal. Or you hide and bury your reactions.
This is probably healthier because it is almost impossible to
straighten out the ambiguities of irritation, not, at least, without a lot of time. Often he is an adult—parent, teacher—
who feels he has legitimate social authority over you. In this
case, it is the legitimacy of his authority which is the final
torture: not only is he the slave of his idea, but the idea is
organized and in some ways convincing—it even has points
of conviction and beauty! Yet it is difficult to separate the
power of his persuasion from the coercive shadows of social
authority that hulk behind him, against which his sweet talk
seems hypocrisy.

You recognize the situation? But do you recognize it when
you do it, too? It is a cliché to ascribe ideological and social
blindness to adults—to all people older—but it is worth re-

alizing that this form of torture is constantly employed by children, not simply on each other, but very often against the adults around them. It is a very human form of warfare, and as often as I see arrogant old age throw its weight around, I see young people demanding that their parents conform to their idea of what "parents should be," that their teachers always be "good teachers," that various groups of people must be "enlightened institutions," and carrying these demands to destructive degrees. Youth is no guarantee of innocence, nor age of wisdom.

Is this warfare an inevitable part of the human condition? No. It can be eliminated in a split second. All that is required is the universal realization, of which all people are capable, that real relationships between people are not ideas (they are not systematic), and that they exist most valuably between people who don't ask too much of each other. "The milk of human kindness is less apt to turn sour if the vessel that holds it stands steady, cool, and separate, and is not too often uncorked." [1]

We cannot save the world on a page. What needs saving is ourselves, and in this task we have incomparable resources: each other. If we do not hamper each other with intense personal desires nor try to catch each other in a net of social expectations, we can hope for reciprocal respect and concern. We can only hope. Reciprocity cannot be forced. But it is essential that you recognize it when it begins to occur and respond directly, immediately, to that person. With a few such people you will construct your life.

A N occasion of festive duty: the school is throwing a party for the trustees and the art department, wives in-

[1] George Santayana, *Character and Opinion in the United States* (New York: W. W. Norton and Co., Inc., 1967), p. 171.

cluded. Party and trustees are perennial, but they meet a different department each year. This way the trustees can touch the bureaucratic bases informally, and we teachers can meet them at least once every ten years or so. Perhaps in anticipation of this event, during the preceding two months our department has undergone a mild but official scrutiny of its activities, including an inquisition into the duties of its members. (The context of the inquiry is the suspicion that we are not doing enough for the school—none of us is a housemaster, and few of us coach athletics. Somewhere I still have the schedule I kept, hour by hour, morning, afternoon, and evening, of how I spent my time for two weeks, an effort I made because fact and rumor are mortal enemies: if one wins, the other must lose. I can still manage a flicker of irritation when I compare my carefully recorded sixty-five-hour week of classes, course preparation, and activity supervision with the school stereotype of the art teacher as a selfish slob.) By the time of the party, we are all ready to bury the hatchet for good, with the benignant blessing of the trustees.

I look over my small collection of dress clothes and select the heavy, black wool suit. As I lift it out of the closet and strip it off its hanger, I delight in its texture and its weight: it will certainly tame the early spring chill, and more important, signal something special to those who are accustomed to my normal casualness of dress. This is a suit with a pedigree, a most dignified hand-me-down!

(My father bought it in 1924, hand-tailored in New Haven, to celebrate his hard-won graduate degree, a uniform for his induction into the foreign legion of academia, more than miles distant from the tiny Texas mule ranch where he had been born thirty years before. The path between had led a circuitous route through a small local college, into the air force—the Armistice fell just at his training's end—to a critical fork: one path led to a conditional enrollment at Yale [they could not imagine what his education could have

been], and the other, via a service friend's offer, to a job as
foreman on an oil field. He risked everything on an almost
accidental childhood love of poetry and came north. Five
years later, he felt he had earned a new suit. I never saw him
wear it; he brought it out of some time capsule and gave it
to me when I graduated from design school: an almost
brand-new but ancient diploma, smelling of moth balls,
which I could not assume without refitting—I had inherited
shorter legs, and he had grown broader shoulders behind a
plow. The tailor I took it to was old, and his age made him
choosy. He was in the midst of refusing the job when he noticed that the fly had buttons rather than a zipper, and he
changed. "Now that's a suit!" he said, fondling and hefting
the material. "They don't make them like that any more.
See, buttons on the fly. They knew what was right!" and he
did the job for the suit, not for me; but when he was done,
it did fit me—the first suit that ever did.)

Putting on the suit is an act of self-defense. If one's appearance is neat and circumspect, mildness can endure a social brawl. I decorate its dull black armor with the green
and red tartan necktie given me by my wife's clan at our
wedding, and my security is complete. I am adrift in feelings
of historicity as I wait for Sue to finish dressing, and we start
walking slowly up the street to the party.

(My historical musings are sparked by one-day-old memories of my father's puffed, gray face which I found over the
raised rail of a hospital bed. Surprise and delight lit his eyes
as he said, "Hello, brother" toughly, and protested that I
shouldn't have come, that he would be out soon, and I was
nervous not to excite him because his heart is wounded and
I didn't know whether it is only pain and worry that can kill
it. I had not seen him in the five days since his thrombosis,
and he was a cruel sight. His hand, as he grasped mine, was
moved by spirit rather than muscle, the same spirit that had
generated his refusal to be carried from the house to the am-

bulance in the evening's air: if he was in pain and dying, it
was his life still, and he would not submit to public minis-
terings. He walked out on his own.

We chatted with a lightness carefully maintained, he of his
condition—I was not to worry—and me of my work admin-
istering the construction of a new elementary school, which
had kept me away until then. Even though we were both
teachers, we remained friendly foreigners, a fact of mutual
accommodation and on his part, intention: he could never
have recreated his origins for me, though he could tell tales
about them; and although he occasionally glimpsed my life,
he could barely begin to understand what our differences,
which he had earnestly earned, meant. He had let me be,
and it was from a psychological distance that I had watched
him slowly give up his life to that deadliest of traps, an educational institution. He, the teacher, had taught me, the
teacher, that we teachers are the most perniciously harried
middlemen that ever existed. All miracles are asked of us as
daily duty, and the rewards are small, few, and far between.
Even simple gratitude is sparse. The teacher's greatest gift to
a student—independence—is best given in disguise, so that
the student feels he has done it all himself and can walk
away without looking back. As for administrators, they seem
happiest when they are not forced to know what a teacher is
doing: the ship of state has not been rocked. Yet in this
strange country, education is god, and his emissary, the
teacher, is supposed to change our populous unleavened
dough into the wonder bread of success. A bitter business.
Yet I had learned from him. I did not expect miracles and I
knew, somewhat, the price I would be asked to pay, and was
prepared. Dad had been caught by surprise, and had fought
back only with gentleness, while his sweet yeast turned
slowly bitter, and he was consumed as he was used. The
image of his wasted body came away with me.)

The party is in plenary session when we get there, a loud

mixture of familiar and unfamiliar faces. Sue and I spot a slightly isolated group of older people who are talking quietly, and sit down with them. The older of two trustees is talking with the other's wife about the U.S.S. *Pueblo,* which had been captured five days earlier. She has just observed some of the international complexities of the issue. The gray-haired man snorts, and declares, with the calm smile of a man of the world, "Well, I think we are being misled by all this pussyfooting around. What we should do is drop an atom bomb on one of their smaller cities. And if they don't give the ship back, drop another, and keep going until they do. That way, they'll know who they're dealing with." He leans back to share with us his perception of power.

(Within three seconds I am totally, fiercely, coldly angry. The enemy has declared himself, in full view, flaunting and flourishing his arrogance. In the name of all who have suffered, are suffering, and will suffer because of such power, and for whom I have donned my black armor, I will tilt at him: he is no windmill. Overland two thousand miles, overtime seventy years, I bring a message from the mule ranch. My stroke is swift and civilized, aimed at the vitals.)

"That is the most *irresponsible* statement I have heard anyone make—*anyone*—since I came here six years ago!"

(He cannot mistake the intensity of my voice, nor the fierceness of the gesture with which I indicate how many "anyones" I mean, but he cannot know the enormity of the charge. He has not spent six years with large numbers of adolescents, whose innocence, attacked by social stress, leads them to say the damnedest things, to inflict wanton pain without the slightest awareness of the effect. He has not endured six years of faculty meetings, a medium designed to hide sensitivity to truth under a rhetoric of "responsibility," while any idiot knows that rhetoric is, by its nature, irresponsible. The best things are done when least is said, but this does not often happen. Nor has he lived in a private school community, a place where the art of gossip is relished and carried to extraordinary distances from reality, just for the hell of it. Well, many students grow up, all faculty meetings come to an end, and it is self-evident that a gossip is—by definition—a person of ill repute. But trustees are supposed to be trusted!)

But never mind, I will talk only about those people he has stated his willingness to destroy so casually. What do they have to do with the U.S. Navy? As I make this point, he gets up. Maybe he listens to my speech, but when I finish, he leans down and looks me in the eye. His voice is harsh, angry.

"Buddy-boy, I can see that you and I are not going to agree." And he stalks away.

(One can be angry and right at the same time only a few times in one's life. As I realize that our exchange has been successful, that we have understood each other, and that his leaving while I stay amounts to a public confession, my anger is gone, and I enter a long, animated chat with the woman, who seems not the slightest put out by having been so brusquely interrupted.)

My father has another mild attack that weekend, and the following Wednesday, early in the morning, he dies.

(Not all important things are parenthetical.)

2 **Given a sense of relationship between two people, the form of their communication is largely determined by the perception each has of the distance between them; the success of their dynamic interchange depends on their agreement on the nature and size of that distance.**

The key word here is *distance*. It is clearly related to the notion of independence in the first statement, but goes a step further, suggesting: (1) that there are differing degrees of independence possible between two people; (2) that at any time the degree is actual rather than vaguely "possible"; (3) that in our relationship with another we constantly judge our degree of independence; and (4) that the judgment we make is the most important shaper of what we do and say to each other.

You and I are going to have trouble with this word "distance," precisely the same trouble each of us has day in and day out with any person, even one with whom we are familiar: we understand him and we do not understand him. Bear with me. I shall have to dance a few rings and "suppose," as Frost has it, while "the Secret"—in this case the meaning of distance—"sits in the middle and knows." [2] I will start, as a first turn, with what we can see happening between people: an objective view of *physical distance*. After that, I will try to discuss some of the more direct aspects to us, as we live and interact within each other's *experiential distance*.

PHYSICAL DISTANCE

Let me conjure up two ghostly visions in your mind which, in their extramental impossibility, define the limits of distance. First, you are watching two people talk together, and as their mutual ease and shared assumptions grow, they approach each other, and before your eyes, begin merging: each overlays the other, they bypass their boundaries, and molecule by molecule, atom by atom, are combined. Where in every case there were two, now there is one, and by some continuous transmutation both are synthesized into some new, single creature. All prior differences have disappeared, distance has become zero. Second, you are watching two people talking together, and as they disagree and irritate one another, their mutual repulsion grows, and before your eyes, they are forced apart: soon they disappear from the earth,

---

[2] From *The Poetry of Robert Frost* edited by Edward Connery Lathem. (New York: Holt, Rinehart and Winston, Inc.)

then from the solar system, the galaxy, the universe, and after a very long time you suppose that they no longer have any effect on each other, and that their mutual forgetfulness is complete. All prior differences have disappeared, distance has become infinite.

Two dreams that never come true. Even incest falls far short of the first mark, and as for the second, even death does not us so part. No, all human exchange takes place somewhere between these two extremes, in the land of the dangerously ordinary. As we watch these two people converse across our supper table, as they touch each other off, their eyes begin to shine, and their new animation blesses our meal, we *see* the distance between them: it is lit by candles which nod and toss with every breath and gesture, and move the shadows around the scarred wooden surface. This dead space between them is brought to life by the differences it begot: their words never coincide, their gestures never meet, their faces never mirror, nor their accents echo. Our passive pleasure is driven by their separation, our attention is fascinated by their differences: when one gives, the other takes; when one is stubborn, the other bends; when one blasphemes, the other blesses. There is no rope between them, yet they tug. Their pleasure is not ours but, as they go at it, they give us something to understand. What can we guess about them, what can we see? Let us lean back and look with a cold eye.

PERCEPTUAL DISTANCE

Since these two people, as any two at any time, exist in different places, the information in the sensory field of each is different. By extension, the totality of sensory experience, over all time, is different for each. In a functional situation, this means that each will see each other, a mutual problem, a job to be done, anything intermediate, differently. The degree of difference is not determined solely in terms of the information each has and gets, no part of which, much less the totality, can, for the two of them, be identical. More important is where they "meet" on a scale, the poles of which are, at one end, the strength and completeness with which each pays attention to his own perception of the other person and the intermediate task, and at the other end, the need of both to agree on what the intermediate task *is,* simply in order to decide what each will do. Agreement is bought at the price of each ignoring large parts of his perceptual field—and this price is paid equally in the hot-air-filled political forum, the courtroom's severe tension, the quiet sanctity of the physics laboratory, or the free-for-all of the dinner table. This selective, and sometimes repressive, move toward compromise is not, in itself, communication. The strength of communication between two people is determined by the awareness each has of the compromise the other is constantly making, an appreciation of the other's struggle, and the willingness each has to enter that struggle. Marshall McLuhan's maxim to the contrary, the medium is *not* the message: the experience of communication occurs *within* people, in a region of utter darkness from which they grope toward each other.[3]

CULTURAL DISTANCE

Perceptual distance is defined, at one pole, by the strength and totality of the attention each person pays his unique and immediate sensory field. Cultural distance is defined, at a corresponding pole, by the strength and totality of the fidelity each person pays his remembered experience—his faithfulness to his origins and his extended environment. Each has experienced different times and places. A person's most significant history is made up of his commitments to and ac-

---

[3] At least one interpretation of McLuhan's perverse statement might be that it suggests, in its focus on the medium, that we simply ignore what we cannot know—all the hidden, internal complexities of human exchange—and do no supposing.

ceptances of what is true about himself and the world. Any compromise of that history is a compromise of truth. The value and strength of communication does not depend on sacrificing truth, but on holding some of it in abeyance, maintaining its strength in silence, allowing it to inform and shape a new truth, the truth of the present moment. Between two people at that moment their realistic relationship depends on their mutual acceptance of their cultural distance which, in its complexity, is at least as diverse as their perceptual distance. In fact, as each maintains his integrity, his personal history affects his perceptions enormously. The main issue between the two people is the willingness of each to create new, intermediate truth—a never-ending labor obscured only by habit.

MOTIVATIONAL DISTANCE

In that the source of his action and the change from contemplation to motion occurs within him, each person seeks different satisfactions and moves in that seeking differently. It is easy to guess that these differences are closely connected to differences of perception and personal history, yet this connection, besides being intimate, is also intricate and full of new possibilities of variation. The change from deliberation—in which each mulls over his perceptions and past—to decision—in which each chooses to do something beyond his person in the present and so make a message—is a *total* change, and in the moments of its occurrence is open to many influences, some conscious, some unconscious. All combine to suggest that each person has an organically total purpose which we sense strongly as his own, as belonging to him, and as we watch two people work together, even if their coordination, cooperation, and evident mutual pleasure are strong, we are still aware of each as a separate generator, and that their success is brought about not so much by the alternation, between them, of submission and initiative

as by their efficient use of each other's energy. Some of the
most powerful and stable achievements are by people who
differ in their goals, in their deepest notions of reality, but
who are willing to work together on a common task.

METHODOLOGICAL DISTANCE

Another important difference, closely involved with the
preceding three, is in the way two people go about doing
something, and in particular, doing something together.
When a person tackles a problem, either one of direct communication, or of his getting a job done—and the two are
often synonymous—his approach is unique, partly because
he sees the problem uniquely, partly because his previous
experience of reality is unique, partly because his desires are
unique, but also because his ongoing interaction with the
problem is unique: his trials and his errors can be shared
only after he has made them, and either his hand has been
bitten or his back patted. Two people can very strongly
agree on a common goal and immediately have all kinds of
trouble coming to terms on how to reach it—honest trouble,
even uncorrupted by politics. We watch them argue inter-
minably, even violently, circling round and round, each
trying to preserve the integrity of his pragmatic vision and
his hard-earned habits. The more important and urgent the
problem and the stronger the desire of both to solve it, the
more difficult it is for either to take the indirect steps, the
longer-seeming, sideways-walking steps necessary to evolve a
new method, which must synthesize the experience of both.
As in other cases, communication occurs not because either
person compromises or bastardizes his own integrity, but because each recognizes in addition and wants to use the integrity and strength of the other's experience. It is essential for
both to realize that the new method, grown out of cooperation, can belong wholly to neither alone, and for this reason,
exists beyond the understanding of either. This fact under-

scores the need for each to donate his personal vision unadulterated, accepting the inevitability of conflict and mutual
change: so long as both remain honest *and* adaptable, a
cooperative method gains great strength, stability, and adaptability from their bipolarity.

TEMPORAL DISTANCE

As a final correlative of physical distance between two people, we see and feel the pervasive and many-faceted move-
ments of time as within it things happen between them. On
a small scale but immediately, drastically influential, each
has a different rhythm of thought and action, uniquely
changing, a different rate of reaction, a different sense of
where, in time, the two are in the development of their relationship, and how fast things should develop further between them. On a broader scale, differences of age, different
sense of urgency underlying their mutual activity, different
judgments of how long various kinds of jobs take or need in
order to be done well—all these separate the two. In still
broader terms, the two may differ in their historical perspective, in their attitudes toward change and rate of change, in
their profoundest internal sense of connection with the
ongoing motion of the universe. As with other differences,
successful communication is not a matter of the two falling
into step and marching in some formal but meaningless parade in which each ignores his own drummer. The issue is
one of mutual sensitivity and counterpoint: can the two together act out a music of more complex and surer rhythm
than each could alone?

These five aspects of physical distance and the ways we see
others cope with them are continuously and organically involved: the dancers are separate, but they cannot be separated from the dance. To us as spectators their approaches
and withdrawals, their hits and misses, the congruences and
incomprehensions are much clearer than to either of them

and form a temporary totality of what, to them, may appear fragmentary and nonsensical. Before we enter that kaleidoscope world of direct experience and try to make some livable sense of it, let me make one final use of this clarity. Between any two people the distance is finite and variable, no matter how they perceive it—even in situations of almost supernatural accord. As small gaps are actual so are great gaps: they can be crossed, too. The only deterrents are ignorance, delusion, fear, inattention and unwillingness, all of which are matters of choice, not necessity. Communication—powerful, significant, constructive—is always possible, and the world is full of beings who are closer to us than our unchoosing leads us to assume.

EXPERIENTIAL DISTANCE

If our objective view insists that distance between people exists, our experience insists that it varies. When we watch two others, we can see their physical distance but only deduce other differences between them, which remain internal to them. Their differences are only the symptoms of their actual but invisible intersubjective distance. The lines of their communication can never be tapped, although we can hear and watch the messages flicker back and forth. We can sense the nature of their relationship, be it casual or intense, faithful beyond temporary change or strangely brittle, emotional or lucid. But it is only when we—you or I—are directly involved with another person, when our communication is alive, that we enter the intense actuality of what I mean by distance. In this actuality suddenly, immediately, everything about the other person *counts:* the relationship involves willy-nilly the totality of each of us.

Great ranges and changes of emotion catch you up in your counting: fear, love, need, guilt, forgiveness, gentleness, greed, generosity, irritation, jealousy, timidity, aggressiveness, toleration, joy, curiosity, urgency, boredom, revelation, pleasure, conspiracy, success, trust, antagonism, betrayal, fatigue, animation, hope, fulfillment, pickiness, pain, confusion, concealment, tenderness, moral fervor, shared immorality, privacy, publicity, intimacy, coldness, suspicion, freedom, frankness, simplicity, complexity—my God, the list is endless. Surely it is sane to wonder, first, *why* all these buffeting fluctuations occur, and second, how any relationship can survive their interminable variation? Their changing feels so rarely intensely good and frequently only bothersome, tiresome, and intensely disturbing. Are they, after all, to be trusted?

These emotions, as they grip you and shake your soul, are facets of your total perception of the distance of the other person, a totality which unifies into actuality—into the reality to which only emotions can commit us—the two basic, obvious, and antagonistic aspects of distance: separation and connection. To you the other person is independent yet matters, and you the same to him. That actuality is dynamic, its motions within you are energized by distance, which is only synthetically single. A feeling of trust, for example, is energized by the possibility of being betrayed, generosity by the twinges of greed it overcomes, and suspicion is directed most fiercely at him you would most like to trust. In other words, your perception of the other's distance is constructed, and because you are reaching out to the other in tremendous ignorance—an ignorance which is constantly renewed—your constructed perception constantly changes. In this construction you contribute everything of yourself, which includes equally what you reveal, what you hide, what you join, what you slash apart, and—by far the largest area—what you simply leave unconnected. All the while you are building within you this perception of the other's distance, he is doing the same within him. It is *not* that you are building a bridge between you, a viaduct through which you can pour your feelings back and forth, but that you are establishing a mutual perception. The goal is not unanimity nor even compatibility, but a perceived actuality which, like any other part of actuality, appears different from different points of view. The points of view of two people involved in a mutually recognized confrontation are, in fact, opposed.

Perhaps this direct opposition is enough to explain the fluctuations in your experiential relationship with another: it is certainly an unstable configuration, if for no other reason than the fact that each of you is relying on information that the other cannot have about himself. From that hidden withinness of his own, he can—and often does—take you utterly by surprise, disconcerting you, at the least. That this opposition is engendered by distance is obvious. Perhaps less obvious is how each of the emotions listed above is a reflection of your response to distance, although the separation-connection paradox is certainly powerful enough to energize them and many more. By its nature, a paradox commits us to alternating, contradictory truths. Other paradoxes further destabilize the state of your relationship. For example, you contain within you, in unified potential, the mutually exclusive states of initiation or passivity, attention or inattention, concern or coldness, sympathetic and gentle imagination or obsessive, literal-minded demand, anger or placidity. All alternate as clearly appropriate responses, yet each—which totally cancels its opposite—seems often to occur spontaneously, with only tenuous connection to circumstance, and to fulfill, by the nature of its peculiar momentum, only its own prophecy. Boredom, for example, maintains itself against all reason—despite our tendency to blame it on anything but ourselves—and reflects at every moment our desire to remain uninterested. And then it ends, not because something excites us, but because we have become ready to be excited. Perhaps, as we begin to look for sources of stability in relationships, we should wonder if each of these emotions *produces* in some way its opposite in some kind of natural balance, a restorative realism, enhancing stability rather than destroying with its change.

How does a relationship between two people survive its emotional variations? It is fair to start by saying that many don't. In the twists and turns of an expanding mutuality, there is no guarantee that its strength will survive. We are all frail creatures, and are not always able to contain the instabilities I have mentioned, or to resolve the paradoxes of distance. Further, we are capable of all kinds of errors and misjudgments, and of fouling our cleanest perceptions of each other with all sorts of illusions, delusions, preconceptions, self-pity, self-justification, ambition, and manipulation. On the other hand, if we keep our eyes clear and our senses open, and do our best to avoid abuses, mutuality has a much better chance of surviving and growing.

In your mutuality, the other person is your mirror, but his reflection plays many more complicated and puzzling tricks than right-left reversal. When two mirrors face each other, they reflect not each other but their reflections of something intermediate, in an infinite regression limited only by their absorptive and diffractive imperfections. Although in your penetrability and internality the both of you are different from two highly polished surfaces, you and another do share a necessary condition: you must face each other in order to reflect each other. Beyond this, your mutual reflections—your exchanged messages—are mirrorlike. They are not instantaneous, and the information exchanged is not unmixed: one of the most difficult demands of your relationship is to determine when a statement or gesture of the other is giving you significant new information about him, when it is actually information about you, or when it is clearly about both. At all times your image returns having undergone drastic changes: his selectivity destroys some of you, his amplification distorts others of your aspects beyond recognition. In fact, the reflection he gives you is not of you.

You are not "seeing yourself through his eyes"; you are, in an essential way, seeing only him. He stands in the way of your reflected image, and the accuracy and significance of any self-image you derive from him is totally dependent on the accuracy and significance of your image of him. And so both of you are under the sword. Since every deviation is so amplified, it is easy to understand the fragility of a human relationship: even a small nudge can break its connection with personal truth. On the other hand, even though your returned image be undecipherable or hidden from consciousness, or take unexpected turns, if you have any sense of reflection from him, you also reflect him back, and instantly mutuality exists—or reexists. It is just here that honesty—of the kind that strives for totality, not simply for abrasive partiality—and receptivity—unbiased and open—become clearly indispensable to a continuing relationship. Your sharpest and most discriminating nerve-ends and instincts are tuned to judging honesty and receptivity in another person, as are his: you cannot use the other as a mirror simply to primp before.

What is it that straightens your mutual distortions, that resists repulsion, penetrates politeness, circumvents rudeness, ignores pretensions, gentles shyness, pressures you to move toward the other if he seems remote, extricates you from premature intimations of intimacy? Not knowledge, not conscious commitment or unconscious assumption, not naive trust or sophisticated sensitivity. No, you are bound by the alive totality of your being, your internalized sense of actuality. Despite all ebbing and flowing of feeling, despite all variations and permutations of love and hatred, of intense attention and unworried unconcern, you and the other are always *actual:* you can always rely on that, even in moments of utter silence or inattention.

From time to time you experience moments of extraordinary communion with another person, when you feel some sort of profound agreement. Your perceptions may differ, but within that moment anything can happen—freely and unexpectedly—without threatening your sense of peace. At such rare times, your covert agreement and your undeniable trust are unstated (and unstatable), nonrational, and *accurate*. Your separation, your mutual independence are no longer principles, they have become concrete. Your words, gestures, and actions establish and reinforce the particularity of your relationship. You have agreed that your connection is of a certain strength, neither more nor less, and that it can survive the stress of disagreements or demands of certain strength, neither more nor less. Although it is a mistake to think of such moments as achievements, since so much of their content is totally beyond consciousness, they can be sought, and seeking helps. Your search is indirect, not for the pleasures of control but for the conditions of coincidence.

If you are aware of the other only within the context of his distance, then what you ask of him and what he asks of you are less likely to be too much, nor to appear indifferent.

Indifference is the casual and deadly enemy of communication. It defends you against the sometimes threatening demands of personal relationship, but it also hides the fact that personal commitment to another person involves a drastic change of state: when the infinite possibilities of communication have become actual—when you have approached the other person—they have also become finite. You can no longer daydream. You are forced to confront his limitations and your own. Only through the eye of that needle can you begin to enjoy your mutual wealth.

The energy of connection is channeled by your honesty and receptivity, and stabilized by your confidence in the other's honesty and receptivity. Given these conditions, you can trust each other, but more important, you can trust the actuality of the two of you together. Whatever happens, it includes the two of you, and is vitally real.

Let me return, at last, to the initial statement, which has two parts. The first part says that the form of two people's communication is largely determined by the perception each has of the distance between them. I hope that this is obvious even though we don't think about it much. What I am insisting on—and you may not realize the strength of my insistence, and have no way of testing the stubbornness with which I will defend the idea—is the *priority* of this perception. Our perception of mutual distance precedes and is the constant context of anything that happens between us, and affects, with unconscious and total power, not merely *how* we say and do things with each other, but *what* we say and do. In other words, not only are our methods of mutuality selected and shaped by our sense of distance, but our personal purposes are intricately adapted to it. The distance between us is where we begin with each other—it precedes our beginnings with each other—and therefore our distance is the first reliable aspect of our relationship. When we first begin to trust each other, that trust is subsequent to and dependent on our mutually perceived distance: before we attempt in any way to cross the space between us we must have acknowledged that the space exists.

This perception runs contrary to other suppositions, some of which start with a notion of free will, or at least of independent personal intention as an actual (although subjective) experience, others of which enmesh themselves in ideas of an organic universe of inescapable causality. I am saying here that our perception of distance and mutual independence, because of its actual precedence in our perceptions, is a constraint, a force toward order—toward an order of actuality rather than toward an idea of order. Our perception of distance precedes and controls even the wildest ideas of anarchy.

On the other hand, because it is nonrational, unstatable, and of varying accuracy, our perception of distance and mutual independence guarantees, by the power of its precedence, that any idea of the truth of human relationships or any attempt to force them into and hold them in a permanent mold is bound to be superceded. The order of actuality actually changes. Our actuality precedes our perception of actuality, and it is by accepting this precedence that we can help each other toward the finite freedom that is our birthright. In this attempt, our relationships with each other are both stable and capable of change.

The second part of the statement says that two people's successful interchange depends on their agreement on the nature and size of the distance between them. Again, I am stubborn on the matter of precedence. Successful communication is not contained within the exchange of messages. Rather, it is dependent primarily on the context of perceived distance, and secondarily on the sensitivity with which each person senses that distance changing and adapts his actual responses to that change—whether that change be an approach, a withdrawal, or a carefully maintained constancy. Only after these happen can the subtleties of the message begin to bear. The priority of our perception of distance suggests a direct contradiction to more ordinary assumptions which suppose that communication is inversely proportional to distance itself: that our strongest communication is with those to whom we are most intimate, while the weakest occurs between those who are farthest away. We presume much in our everyday life and language to suggest the truth of this assumption. Part of the presumptive pressure is circumstantial: we have more contact with people who are closer. Part of it is illusory: we assume, on the basis of habit, that we are communicating with people who are close to us when, in fact, we aren't. Part of it is laziness: it is easier to "agree" with these closer people simply to maintain our social comfort. But all of these presumptions are obvious errors, and do not withstand an analysis of the necessities of life or of survival. In the first place, as I have tried to show, communication cannot be equated with agreement about messages exchanged: without the prior perception of distance, the messages can have no substantial meaning, and therefore can be the vehicle for no substantial agreement. Rather than assuming that the strength of communication is inversely proportional to distance, it is more important to realize that we can entertain strong, successful communication even at great distance. That distance may be temporal as well as spatial. What is required for us to cross it is our actual participation in the actuality of that distance.

HECTOR BERLIOZ, you old devil.

You can buy the album if you want, and if you have a hi-fi, follow James Agee's instructions: lie down and put your head near the speaker with the volume on full. You may get a glimmer—at long range still even though the noise sounds in the center of your head—of some full-blown intent, a wandering whirlwind of startling sounds and violent reminders of sentiment. But even if you manage a clearheaded attention and a constant receptivity, you will get only an inkling the first time through. I know. I was there, buried in the chorus through the rehearsals, the performances, the recording session, until the grooves of that celebratory, ritual, and sacrificial sound seemed etched on my skin. Performers perform for themselves and each other; an audience can listen in, and if it is lucky and the performers are good, some of the energy of the exchange leaks out— some, but not all. Even less of it passes through the electroplastic recording process. So come, let me be your Mephistopheles, pick you out of your tracks and carry you back into that experience of mine. Layer by layer let me unwrap it so that you can weep in its pungency and savor, on your tongue, its heart.

The Damnation of Faust by Berlioz, performed by the Boston Symphony Orchestra, Charles Munch conducting, with the Harvard-Radcliffe Glee Club, G. Wallace Woodworth, conducting. Soloists: David Poleri as Faust; Suzanne Danco as Marguerita; Martial Singher as Mephistopheles. An RCA monaural recording, LM-6114. So much for names. They form a thin, dry brown skin, to be discarded.

The people—three hundred strong—are an assortment you could nowhere match for diversity: of age, of continental origin and accent, of musical skill, of pure physiognomy. The chorus, all young, is still as diverse as men and women are, collected from across the nation and then some, covered in various thicknesses of cultural overlay depending on their years in Cambridge and their honesty, their impetus toward imitation and the social uses they make of it. Beneath, an energetic, questing group, prodigal in its enjoyment of life and feeling blessed by the music. And of course, it is the mating season.

The orchestra, in addition to its instrumental virtuosity, is a college of age and anatomy. A young, suave Boston rake sits next to a tiny, doddering mouse who wears his white halo of hair à la Vienna 1912. A few enthusiasts dance their instruments through the music; others chew gum, look bored, and observe the ten-minute breaks with unionesque ennui. Here is a self-contained society, shaped by competence and competition, a machine for music, which when idling, grumbles to itself in English, German, French, Italian, Hungarian, but when directed, swings into raw, full symphonic sound, the uncommon language of superhuman love.

In a small semicircle at the feet of the conductor, standing when they sing, sit the three soloists. Faust is a young man who dresses with intense casualness for rehearsal: open-collared, short-sleeved shirt, blue slacks. He spends some of his break time chatting with the girls in the front row of the chorus. We basses speculate briefly what he wants from them. Whatever his motives, he sings well; his voice is large and smooth, and his French has a touch of the amateur, enough to suggest that Faust is not a professional alien. Marguerita is older, smaller. The innocence she conveys is a subtle, highly informed, *experienced* innocence: she knows what the stakes are in ways that the girl in the story did not (or only learned after). Her voice is full of warm nuance, fully French. I fall in love at-a-distance with her every time she stands up and I can see her. Mephistopheles is in his forties, balding, with the capacity to raise his eyebrows to the top of his skull when his sophistication is outraged—as it often is by Faust's naive pursuit of happiness. His voice is rich, operatic—and again, French in its subtle inflections. He obviously enjoys playing the devil, as I'm sure the devil would, and his pleasure becomes outright, arrogant joy when he entraps Faust. His change from sycophantic servant to merciless soul-grabber is the most dramatic and skillfully suggested change in the entire production.

At the center stands Munch, the conductor, a tall, large-headed man whose handsome face, lined and circled with age, speaks more than his halting English. He sways back and forth as we go, not with the beat but with the phrase, seeming always about to fall; but his eyes are self-assured, his will clearly focused at the tip of his long baton: its slightest motion speaks. He finds his way through the mysterious tempo changes without misstep, making musical and emotional sense out of notational mishmash, shaping the drama with the assurance of a—wizard? Rumors of his wild youth and extradomestic dalliances (probably invented for the occasion), which whisper through the chorus backstage, only serve to enhance his personal power when we face it. For the time being, he is Larger than Life. With the simple tools of beatific smile and silent reproach, he teaches us Berlioz.

And what does Berlioz teach? Well, he doesn't. In the first place, he isn't present. I don't mean he's dead and buried. I mean, as we bomb along, three hundred strong, exerting our way through this complicated score, we are transported to a place somewhere else, at some other time, that just might be in Berlioz' head. And if it were, and we have become, temporarily, phantasmic elements of his creative thought, then he cannot be present to us any more than we are present to our thoughts: it is the other way around. But of course, that's a bunch of romantic twaddle—even if the surrounding life of his music, as our skins tingle with its vibrations, makes the illusion likely.

If there is any lesson, it lies in the story. Berlioz wrote the text himself, and I am unsure of its closeness to Goethe's version of the legend. At the start, Faust is in a mood of emotional isolation from nature and the company of men: even the tremendous, driving color and tempo of a full-orchestral military march (a musical tour de force painted in broad strokes of trumpet, trombone, and tuba) leave him insensible (although it invariably brings an audience to its feet). He is about to drink his suicide with a cup of poison when he is halted by the sound of a choir singing in a nearby church. Recollections of childhood religion temporarily stay his hand, and in the midst of his musings, Mephistopheles appears, promising to renew his joy in life. Faust agrees to let him try, so off they go. First to a bar full of rowdy drunks: Faust is unimpressed. The Devil then puts him to sleep and fills his head with beautiful dreams, among them a vision of Marguerita, whom Faust—drugged or hypnotized —immediately falls in love with. When he wakes, with her image permanently present to his mind, the Devil says he

will take him to Marguerita in the flesh. By this time, Faust
is eager. When Marguerita, who has been waiting in an innocent virginity for something to happen to her life, sees
Faust, she too recognizes a dream come true, and they fall
into each other's arms: in a climactic duet they play out
their love over what must be one of the most literal portray-
als of orgasm in the history of music. *"Je meurs,"* sighs Marguerita at the end, the conventional euphemism for sexual
climax peculiarly foreboding.

Mephistopheles bursts in and drags Faust away: the neigh-
bors are aroused and warn Marguerita's mother that her
daughter is in danger. Rapidly all draws to an end. First, we
hear Marguerita sing her weary despair: Faust has been gone
days, weeks, and she realizes that he will not return. Mephistopheles returns to Faust and promises to take him back to
Marguerita if he will sign his name on a piece of parchment.
Totally distracted, by this time, Faust agrees, signs, and
without much delay, the Devil rides him off to hell. Faust
falls screaming into the boiling pit. The drama ends as the
chorus sings of Marguerita's ascent to heaven.

The emotional progression is clear: boredom leads to extremes in a search for life, instantaneously resolved by the
"perfect" love of the "perfect" woman, followed by total frustration and eternal damnation. The moral implications are
unavoidable: the price paid by Faust for his moment of renewed life is enormous—not simply in his own subsequent
pain, but in the destruction of Marguerita. Her death is preceded by a state of reminiscence, in which her life has become only a dream. The heaven she reaches is simply the last
virtuous vapor of her betrayed purity.

But the music has no moral. In fact, as the music spreads
this tale over three hours of carefully articulated emotions
and wildly experimental sounds, the primary meaning becomes clear: Faust and Marguerita are following the undis-

tracted dictates of a generous nature, and their fate is not to
be eschewed but accepted as the next inevitable condition.
For this is how the music moves, from condition to condition, mood to mood, one complete and self-sufficient state of
being to another. This is what cannot be caught on a record:
when you are in the midst of this enormous, totally surrounding sound, every part of this music constitutes part of
an *actual environment*. It's not that when the flutes over
there warble a song they are imitating birds, and are supposed to remind you of another time and place when you
heard real birds warble. Nor is this punched arpeggio from
the clarinets pretending to be a flight of bats in some imagined twilight zone. No, these flutes warble a real song, these
clarinets are really batty: the musical reality in which they
live is, for the moment, more real than any other can be, and
the truth of this is attested to by the undeniable, irresistible
force of the entire orchestra. This is no substitute for experience: this is a forceful, emotional, total reality which can be
neither ignored nor escaped. It's not just that it's loud (and
at times very large), but that it's complete. All other parts of
one's life become, for the time being, only dreams. Within this sound we do not anticipate, we do not remember,
and yet everything happens at the right time, in the right
sequence, at the right speed to match music and emotion.

And so we move forward to the most intense moments of
the entire experience, when Marguerita sings of the de-
parted Faust, of her longing, of her self-recognized dream
that can only sing. As I sat in the midst of the third performance, and the English horn began playing the introduction
to this song, when it played the first two notes of the second
phrase—an unbelievable ninth—I was overwhelmed by a
sudden and totally strange rush of emotion. And as Marguerita began to sing,

D'amour l'ardente flamme
Consume mes beaux jours;
Ah! La paix de mon âme
A donc fuit pour toujours,
A donc fuit pour toujours!

I was possessed, in full clarity and accuracy of perception, in totality and complexity of feeling, by a mood which I accepted as totally Berlioz, as being a state in which, one hundred years before, he had faced and come to terms with love: a mixture of satiety, futility, joy, pride, and regret with which all men and women recognize the elusiveness, the delusiveness, the beyondness, and unreachableness of love, combined with the recognition and acceptance that they must seek its momentary bounty, beyond reason, and in the face of certain loss be faithful. And all this in a most civilized, thorough way, delightfully distressing, complicated and clear, which was foreign and yet told me much about myself, alien and intimate. I felt totally alone with this message, shocked cold with its unexpected force, yet the feeling involved everybody there in a way that needed no further acknowledgment.

Well, there you have it. I don't suppose it is possible to justify the expense and effort of all that musical machinery by my solitary experience of time travel and telepathy, yet to me it seems legitimate because it was so extraordinary. And I guess it would seem so to Berlioz, who wandered up and down Europe for years just to find a good tuba player, so great was his attention to the details of his intent. He was a perfectionist, and, by God, I got the message!

3   Communication is possible because of the existence of transparency and opacity; the two are mutually

**exclusive, and the strength and clarity of our communication
depends on our careful recognition and use of their distinction.**

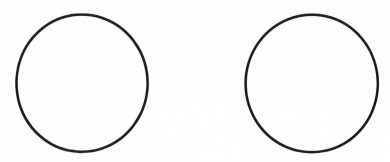

Let the diagram of the two circles represent, in sketch,
two people mutually involved in conversation. The dark
line defining each is his sensory-motor shell as defined above
(pp. 20–22). By drawing these two lines, three regions are
defined: one within each person, and a third outside both.
This last region is the medium through which pass all forms
of energy between them, including those which effect their
senses: certain electromagnetic waves (producing their sensations of light and radiant heat), certain gaseous pressure
waves (producing their sensations of hearing), certain air-
borne chemicals (producing smell), other matter-borne
chemicals (producing taste), and those others which produce
their sensations of heat and cold, of touch and pressure,
of gravitational orientation, of pain, and various other dis-
ruptions of their steady state. The capacity of the interpersonal space to allow these forms of energy to pass through
it is a way of describing its *transparency*. This same space allows us to move through it, and so we habitually think of it
as passive, or even nonexistent (if we think of it at all), but
it is important to realize that things might be different, that
the space might *not* let energy or our more material motions
through, and that since it does, we must see its transparency

as essential. Clearly, if no energy could pass through this space, these two people could not communicate in any sensory way, and in physical terms, the statement above about the necessity of transparency to communication is justified.

What about *opacity*? By opacity I refer to the fact that the energy which "freely" moves through transparent space is stopped and in some way changed at the surface of our material bodies—a surface which is continuous, and closed. For example, in the case of our two people, the ambient light hits the surface of one, where its direction and content are changed (some of it absorbed, some reflected), and *for that reason* some of it reaches the other, specifically the other's eye where, again, it is changed—this time from light to nerve impulses. The light itself penetrates no further. It is easy to see that if these two changes did not occur, one at the surface of each person, they could not "see" each other, and any of their communication which involved seeing could not occur. It is not difficult to extrapolate and extend the need for opacity, so defined, to all of our senses, and so justify the statement about the necessity of opacity to communication.

To this spatial picture I add some temporal distinctions.

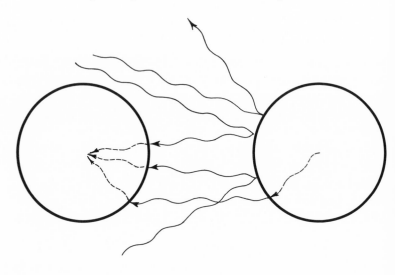

While information is passing through transparent space it cannot contribute to our sensation of time simply because we cannot be aware of it until it reaches us. In this way the passivity of transparency as a spatial concept can be translated into a temporal concept of no-time. That is, as a particle of sensation impinges on a person's surface, it is to him a singular temporal event of no duration, and should be called instantaneous in that it is preceded and followed only by no-sensation. No-sensation equals no-time. Opacity, on the other hand, consists of the totality of instantaneous sensations—instantaneous changes of the surface state of an organism or object. That is, within our experience of time there are no intermediate conditions between change and no-change, although both of these must be present. Our total experience of time combines, in some way, these two conditions—change and no-change—and it seems a small step to say that as communication occurs in time it should, in its operation, alternate between these conditions.

As a last extrapolation, let the two circles represent any two "things." All energies involved in our perceptions change at their surfaces. All surfaces are opaque. Likewise, the space between two "things" is transparent. And in time, all relationships between "things" alternate between change and no-change. If you grab a piece of world, large or small, within its boundaries you will find transparency, opacity, or both. You will not find neither. That is, within the piece energy will pass through all points and will either be seen to change or not to change at each point. Accordingly, each point can be labeled opaque or transparent at that moment. At a later moment, each point is either the same in this respect or different. So defined, opacity and transparency describe a conceptual system to define the condition of any point, hence any set of points. In addition, our perception "tells" us that sets of opaque points form surfaces of "things," each of which encloses itself, and that these "things" are separated by large collections of transparent points which form a continuous space between. Why do our perceptions "tell" us this is so? Can we trust our perceptions in this respect? Is the relationship between conception and perception strong in this case? Do the two together form an unmoving ground on which we can steadily walk?

While you have this objective picture and these questions clearly in mind, let me outline some implications of transparency, of opacity, and of their relationship, in an attempt to show how they can be a basis for perceiving a real relationship between our own physical structure, some aspects of the physical structure of the rest of the universe, our perception of that universe, and our experience of ourselves as real —our self-perceptions. All of these contribute to communication and establish it as trustworthy if we perceive it whole. In broad terms, the following discussion defines (1 and 2) the complementary nature of transparency and opacity, (3) their relationship as we experience them, (4) their infinite nature, (5) their finite combination in actuality, (6) their more direct relationship to acts of communication, (7) their contribution to a theory of being, (8) their relationship to my vocabulary, and (9) their relationship to the conditions of human freedom. In some ways what follows is the heart of my offering to you, and as you dig into it, please remember that the real issue is not whether you trust what I say, but whether I can help you trust yourself, and crucially, trust yourself into survival.

1. Transparency and opacity as defined above are mutually exclusive. Although the term "energy" is common to both definitions, the word is only a vehicle for contrasting them. A more rigorous definition might not use the word or the idea of energy at all.[4] The main thing here is to see the link between transparency and the notion of absolutely-nothing-happening, and the other link between opacity and hap-

[4] For an example, see Appendix II.

pening. Whatever energy *is*—and this is a question that a scientist does not ask because within the assumptions of science it has no meaning—we cannot know because energy does not happen. What *happens* is that energy remains energy, but as it does its work it changes form, or location, or concentration, or orderliness. *Only as it changes* does energy become available to our examination; *only as it changes* does energy become available to our sensations; *only as it changes* does energy become opaque. If nothing happened, if energy did not change form, *if opacity did not exist,* then we would have no basis for assuming that transparency exists, that over time and across space something can remain constant—the unhappening something we call "energy."

2. Just as the clarity of our perception of the mutual exclusivity of transparency and opacity described in this way depends on our perception of their mutual necessity, so our perception of their mutual necessity depends on our perception of their exclusivity. When we say, "energy changes," we are, by words alone, uniting something that is essentially constant (energy) with an idea of motion (change). The assurance of our statement unites two incompatibles and so tempers our idea of either that we cannot conceive of one except in terms of the other. So with opacity and transparency. As we perceive them, they are utterly different yet absolutely necessary to each other—and not simply in the physical terms implied by the use of the word "energy." It is impossible for us, even in the language of imagination or of private vision, to create the thought of a universe in which only one or neither existed. The capacity of energy to move freely is only significant (and imaginable) if combined with the notion that it has an origin or a destination, a "start" or a "stop" where something "happens"—in fact an opaque surface.[5] Without the latter, the idea of energy quickly reverts

[5] Or, more thoroughly, where we can determine that the "energy" has been spent, in accordance with the Second Law of Thermodynamics: that its order

to an idea of nothing: the idea of energy becomes indistinguishable from the idea of pure space, and pure space becomes simply indistinguishable. If, on the other hand, we try to imagine a universe of solid opacity, in which energy, no matter in what direction it moved or over what distance, always instantaneously changed form—so that the constant concept of energy was utterly meaningless, and the concept of meaning or even of concept couldn't exist, because within our heads, it could have no physical constancy—we would be trying to imagine a universe without space, to begin with, and without connection or coherence of any sort. But in reality, our imaginations (which are undeniably part of reality) cannot give reality to either of these possibilities, and in this inability imagination asserts its own reality—which is the basis of our faith in it. Our imagination says that energy must alternate between no-change and change—between the transparent and the oqaque.

In transparency and opacity we have a real *and* abstract example, a perception and a conception of two basic elements which are mutually exclusive and yet totally and undeniably necessary to each other. In other words, we have a conceptual unit by which both mind and world work, in which the real, perceptual connection of exclusive elements is exemplified. Transparency and opacity are separate yet connected. To live with this paradox requires, again, double vision. The possibility of "real" communication is raised: to each other you and I are clearly opaque; can we share the transparency of our conditions? Across the transparent distance between us we flash our oqaque messages. You and I are really separate; can we be really connected, too?

3. If we accept their mutual exclusivity and necessity, the physical relationship between opacity and transparency can be defined in another way (see figure 1): In the illustration,

has decreased, and its entropy increased. We cannot observe this except as energy is transduced and becomes opaque.

which should be considered a magnification of something very small, we see two intersecting directions, labeled 1 and 2, which define a two-dimensional plane. (Please ignore, but only for the moment, the large black circle, which I have drawn for the immediate purpose of establishing the conditions just around the intersection of lines 1 and 2; the following discussion is restricted to that region.) On one side of line 1, at the intersection, the impinging light energy is changed differently from the way it is changed on the other side. On one side is the blackness of the circle, on the other

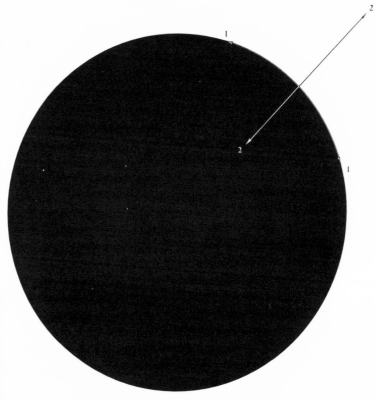

Figure 1

the whiteness of the paper. If we restrict the area of our consideration, we can make it small enough that we have no significant questions about whether this edge (line 1) is a straight line, nor whether, on either side of it, the energy change is uniform. We are considering only the existence of contrast. In this image, we can still clearly distinguish between two directions: the first (line 1, which I have extended outside the circle simply to make my reference visible) runs along the edge, is always black on one side, white on the other, and establishes *where* the contrast occurs; the second (line 2) runs perpendicular to the edge, is either black on both sides or white on both sides, and, as it crosses from black area to white area, by the continuity of its direction and the discontinuity of its condition establishes *that* the contrast occurs or exists. It can be seen that these two directions are mutually exclusive, and before your eyes, mutually necessary. Yet we can see this only because of a second major element, a third direction, perpendicular to the first two, through which can travel the information that this contrast exists and along which, in addition, comes into being our understanding that these first two directions are exclusive and yet bound to each other. This third direction starts at the intersection of the first two and runs from there to the eye of any person actually looking at them, where they "project" an image perpendicular to the third direction: it runs between you and the page. Once you perceive it, you must perceive, too, that this direction passes through you and beyond. This third direction is utterly transparent. Within the space which this third direction establishes occurs our "seeing," but the direction itself—as it exists at all times parallel to our line of sight—cannot be seen. Because this direction (or dimension) is transparent, *and only because it is,* we can "see" the first two directions (or dimensions). Their two arrows are visible because of this third, invisible arrow. In other words, although underlying this diagram is a Euclidean, three-dimensional space, more basic still is the entirely non-Euclidean notion that the three dimensions involved— which are the real dimensions of the world as we perceive it —are *not symmetrical*. The first two together comprise the dimensions of opacity: the first of edge, and the second of contrast. Together, they comprise what is seen (or sensed). The third is the dimension of distance, the dimension of transparency: it is unseen and can only remain unseen.

The three dimensions—of edge, of contrast, and of transparency—are mutually exclusive, entirely different, nonrational in their relationship, and equally necessary to our understanding of the universe.

Three quick sketches of the relationship of the three dimensions so described as demonstrated by (a) our physiology, (b) our experience of emotion, and (c) the operation of intellect:

(a) Physiologically:
1 = Edge = maintained division between adjacent sensory cells
2 = Contrast = difference in reactions of adjacent sensory cells
$1 + 2$ = Opacity = total sensory field, consisting only of contiguous, contrasting nerve impulses
3 = Transparency = external transmission of impinging energy, and internal transmission and eventual mix (or "purposeful" nonmix) of sensory information via central nervous system.

The consistency of our physiological structure and the function of its parts is clear: at *our* "edge," where we contrast with what is not us, exist our organs for measuring contrast and establishing sensory borders; within us, connected perpendicularly to our surface, exists our physiological means of relating to the external world and of hypothesizing its connections with itself. It is as we and the world coexist in three dimensions that we can relate to each other.

(b) Experientially:
  1 = Edge = change, rapid in time, from one recognizable mood to another
  2 = Contrast = difference in the substance and totality between prior mood and present mood
  1 + 2 = Opacity = fragment of emotional "motion" or life
  3 = Transparency = the distance between this fragment and: our understanding of it, our capacity to invest it with meaning, and to relate it to other aspects of our experience, including external events.

All three together form our capacity to react "responsibly" to the world, to respond to changes in our environment and in our feelings in a way that makes sense to us and to our environment; in other words, the three together form our emotional life and its relationship to the world, and thereby are the major variables of our trust of the world and our trust in ourselves.

(c) Intellectually:
  1 = Edge = the acknowledged dividing point between two symbols (e.g. a and b, or a and not-a, or simply a as opposed to the space around it)
  2 = Contrast = acknowledged difference of "content" of these symbols
  1 + = Opacity = the acknowledged "combining" of two disparates (e.g. a + b) into a single "order," as yet without meaning
  3 = Transparency = the space in which to consider the possible meaning (of a + b) and the time in which to construct the meaning.

The three together form an element of an intellectual system by which, in our thinking, we make a commitment to certain differences (e.g. between a and b), and set aside a mental space for each symbol; and at the same time commit ourselves to the relationship between these spaces—that whatever they may contain will be connected, across their separation, by the same relationship, of a to b. In other words, by this act of intellect, we combine absolute distinction (=opacity) with infinite possible meaning of that distinction (=transparency).

I pick these three examples with a purpose. If my argument has convinced you at least of their necessity in some instances, then it will take no further argument to persuade you of their importance to our survival—I remind you of my broadest purpose. If we can trust the combined operations of our bodies, our emotions, and our intellects, I would say that our chances of survival are good. If that trust is only conditional, then we must find out the conditions.

4. In different ways, transparency and opacity each is without limit. Transparency, by its definition, postulates an infinite dimension along which quanta of energy can travel without being changed, without encountering opacity or becoming opaque. Opacity postulates an infinite number of times and places at which an energy-quantum can change. Transparency is beyond measurement, it eludes our senses, and therefore is not rational: our only rational judgment is to consider it limitless. There is no reason, and can be no evidence, not to. Opacity, on the other hand, consists of and constitutes all actual and possible surfaces and sensory fields at any and all times. If we pay attention to even the smallest part of it, we find that it is always capable of providing new information. Opacity is an inexhaustible universe of contrast and change. In its purest terms—of minuteness and precision—contrast and change are its *only* ingredients, and any ideas of constancy or connection are not part of it. When

we call opacity infinite, we do so in a mathematical sense: that there is always another contrast, another change, which can be noticed beyond the sum of past noticings. There is always more world to notice, more existence that can be listed. There can be no "frontier" in the collection of information simply because no ground can be called familiar or known: every "known" piece of the world hides behind the opaque enigma of infinitely more information. Any assumptions about "approximation" or the "almost known" can be totally destroyed at any moment by a single, new fact. Time and sensation are brought together, via opacity, into an infinite progression of disjoint stimuli, of disjoint conditions of the total sensory field. So while transparency is infinitely continuous (one might even call it continuity), opacity is infinitely discontinuous. Clustered around the word "transparency," then, are the words "identity," "continuity," "sameness," "unity," "space," even "connection" and "relationship"; while around the word "opacity" nestle the words "distinction," "contrast," "change," "sensation," "surface," "discontinuity," and "uniqueness." The only consistency that opacity possesses is lent by the fact that each of us is constantly enclosed within a particular sensory field, which he cannot escape. This consistency of our being actual parts of an actual universe is lent us as we are separated by our opaque surfaces, and as we contain an internal transparency.

5. It is only when we think of each in isolation from the other, each as a separate idea, that we can imagine transparency or opacity as being infinite, or rather that their quality of being infinite is significant. Our prior observation that they can never *be* separate in our experience imposes a prior limitation on our experience, that it is finite. The fact that the transparency of our connection to any focus of experience—any actual environment, any object in that environment, any person, even any embodied thought—is limited by its opaque surface absolutely restricts that transpar-

ency: the experience is particular, unique, and thereby isolated from all others (much as you and I are isolated from each other). The fact that our particular, unique sensations of any experience are only possible via a totally unified and continuous transparency at once gives us the capacity to ignore many fragments of sensation, and at the same time, forces us to impose limitations on our considerations—limitations within the continuity of our own capacity for making connections. In other words, given our intention to connect different stimuli into one experience—an intention which is clearly the result of our internal transparency, of our identity, and therefore is an intention which precedes any conscious choice—and given our isolated structure and method of functioning, we can achieve this intended experience only by setting limits to the stimuli we consider, limits on their number, and limits on their separation. This intention is not conscious, but precedes our awareness of the conditions of the world at any moment, and especially what we may think as a result of that awareness: we will at all times order and set limits to our experience, whether we wish to or not. These limitations are both "spatial" in the sense that we exclude, at any instant, large parts of our total sensory field, and "temporal" in the sense that we decide arbitrarily (that is, on some basis outside thought) when an experience starts, what sensations are part of that same experience, and when that experience has stopped—when present sensation no longer belongs to it, but is part of something new. Our experience of whatever—of events, of objects, of "ourselves," of consciousness, of mood, of other people—is *always granular:* our experience is divided into discrete, three-dimensional grains of being. These grains are spatially and temporally finite.

Perhaps it is unfair to buy this important idea here, almost in a footnote. But here is where it belongs, not quite hidden, gradually emerging, a new creature of thought to try its legs, a little wobbly at first and perhaps camouflaged by the remainder of the muck it came from, which coats it thinly in places and sometimes so thickly it is hard to see anything new. The boldest hint here, in this notion of *granularity,* is that it is fundamental to consciousness, to perception, and to action. Our most basic being is, for each of us, *centered in us,* and at the same time, *limited.* At certain extremes our experience can seem to deny this. For example, from time to time we can experience the illusion of a floating freedom, a dreamy, transparent state in which the world and one's consciousness seem very large and totally unified. But something inevitably snaps the trap and "pulls us back to reality," which is to say, pushes us away from the world. At other times we are caught up with frenetic involvements in a sea of opaque sensation, in an irresponsible freedom of instant twitch and flashing lights, when anything goes and is immediately gone. But inevitably we are brought back, sometimes by the glance of convention but more often (and thoroughly) by our own needs of selfhood. Between these two extremes and somehow combining them the separate shapes of our lives take form: shapes in which the central eddies of our floating are squeezed and kneaded into motion by sensation, and our existence demonstrates a personal purpose which is as much a surprise to us as to anyone else. Our generality has become particular, and our particularity has become general. Both can occur at once only because we are always in the process of becoming actual.

I am attempting to prepare you to assume that because our most intimate experience of ourselves is granular that the universe is also granular; and that because when we look at it, we find that the universe may indeed be granular, that we are and will continue to be a part of the universe *only* as we, too, are granular. Our survival will be granular. My experience of the truth of granularity precedes and exceeds reason: my mind and words are left stumbling behind, to understand and explain as best they can.

With that understanding of my purpose and method in mind, let me sidestep and reintroduce another idea which I temporarily left behind, the notion of three-dimensionality. In that discussion I distinguished two dimensions of opacity —edge and contrast—and a third, of transparency. The abstractness of the distinctions between them implies infinite numbers: a universe made up of an infinite number of edges, an infinite number of contrasts, and an infinite space of transparency. But our experience of the universe is *not* infinite, and I am earnestly trying to root the idea of three dimensions in your particular, finite experience, or, rather, trying to show you the roots that it has in them.

Return to the drawing (figure 1). We have reached the point when we must recognize the existence of the large black circle, and at the same time realize that in order for the conditions of edge and contrast—on which this entire discussion has so far been based—to exist in the neighborhood of the intersection of lines 1 and 2, the blackness has to be limited (within the whole circle), contained within a shape (its roundness is arbitrary) which has a single, continuous edge. In other words, within our perceptual system it is physically impossible, emotionally impossible, and intellectually impossible for an edge and a contrast across that edge to exist or be created, where we can both see it and think about it, unless that edge defines a single closed area. As contrast is real, it is finite. As it is finite, it is also at the same time concrete and singular. The singularity of a contrast necessitates the singularity of its complementary edge. Together, contrast and edge define a finite grain of sensation, a unit of opacity, and are synthesized in our perception. At one and the same time that the uniqueness and separation of that two-dimensional grain are established, within its edge it is identified. Within its edge it is assumed to be the same. If, in your desire to disagree, you point to some imperfec-

tions in the ink or some other contrasts within the edge of
this black circle in order to prove the erroneousness of this
assumption, you are simply changing the subject of conversation: you are talking about some other grains of sensation. It
is well to realize, though, that when we assume the identity
of the grain of sensation within its edge, this identity is not
only something it possesses, but it is something which we
give to it. *This gift is the most basic act of communication.*

So much for the necessary synthesis of edge and contrast.
Together they insist that our opaque sensory field is itself
granular in that it is made up of units, each of which is distinct and different from all others and, within itself, identical. Taken all together, they establish one pressurized field
of sensation for each of us, an ever-changing pointillist painting in all sensory modes (see figure 2). What happens when
we reintroduce the third dimension? How does the addition,
here, of the idea of transparency get us closer to reality? We
are forced to a further synthesis which includes us even more
forcefully than did our "donation" of identity to the single
grain of contrast. The complementarity of opacity and
transparency—the absolute, always necessary, mutually exclusive relationship between them—establishes their conti-
guity: an opaque surface can have no thickness and must be
bounded, in either direction perpendicular to its two dimensions, by transparency. We are forced, by our experience of
opacity, to acknowledge the existence of space—a space
which lies on *this* side of the opaque, and *at the same time,*
on the *far* side of the opaque.[6] How so? By our own self-contained demand for our own identity. That is, just as there is
only one way for contrast and edge to be actual—by their
being single and enclosing a finite identity—so there is only
one way for us to entertain the actuality of our total, opaque

---

[6] This space is analogous to our recognition of a time *before* and a time
after a given "event" or "change." Both are acts of imagination, from within
our *own* transparency.

sensory field: by assuming that it, too, is singular and wrapped around a finite, *transparent* identity. We assume our own identity, although that identity—in a three-dimensional universe—must be transparent and therefore *cannot be seen* (even by "ourselves"). This assumption, although the result is so intangible, is the concrete demand of our actuality. Being ourselves consists of making this assumption.

Because our own identity cannot be seen, it is indistinguishable.

Because our own identity is transparent, it is indistin-

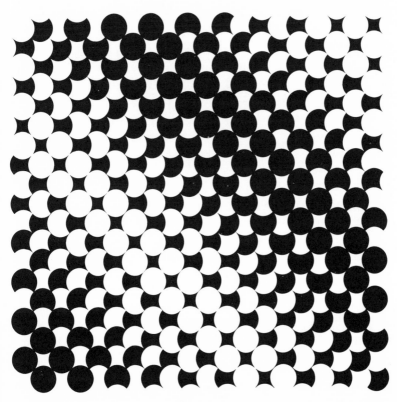

Figure 2

guishable from all other transparency (if transparency can, at any time, be called "other" with any meaning).

In that we recognize the transparency of our own identity —that what we are will at all times elude all definitions except the definition given us by our actuality, our three-dimensional granularity—we must recognize the transparency which lies beyond, on the far side of, our sensations: that there is, indeed, an outside to our existence, but that its first condition, immediately contiguous to us, is transparent. We are forced by the elusive will of our internal identity to interpret our sensations as a continuous, opaque, surface-of-no-thickness-whatsoever, compressed between the transparency of our own identity and the transparency of an exterior space. We are forced to this interpretation because no contradictory evidence can, in total actuality, ever be presented. The fiercer our demand for objective evidence, the more opacity is discovered—and *only* opacity. This simple fact forces us to acknowledge, in contrast, the unavoidable question of identity and transparency: they can be only supposed, but we are forced into this supposition by the indirect actuality of our physical sensations—which are at all times disparate and opaque. That is, it is *only* by paying attention to the outside world that we become ourselves, and *only* in recognizing our own transparent nature that we are forced to confront the dangers and joys of the world's identity. For each of us, his actuality and the world's actuality are coexistent. To see this and be able to act requires our most demanding double vision.

Put this another way. What was, in the two-dimensional field (figure 2), an edge surrounding a unit of contrast (figure 1), now must become, in order to accommodate the reality of the third dimension, a complete, closed surface— itself a unified, opaque field—*enclosing* a transparent volume and *enclosed by* a transparent volume (figure 3). Within this surface, in a manner analogous to our assumption of the identity within its edge of the unit of contrast, we assume the identity of the three-dimensional grain of being: it possesses an "internal" space, consisting of an always hidden transparency, which by its surrounding opaque surface remains always separated from an "exterior" transparency. It is important to note that when I say that the interior space of a grain of being is hidden and transparent, I am saying one thing, not two. *Because* it is hidden we must consider it transparent; *because* it is transparent, it must remain hid-

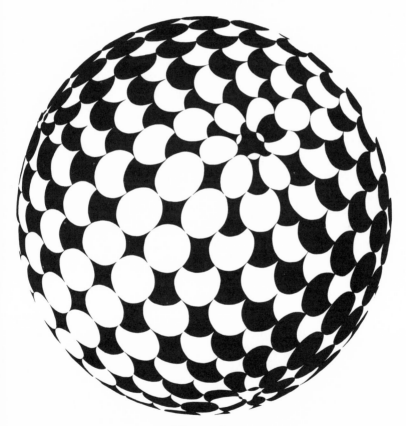

Figure 3

den. All lies beyond the impenetrable sensory shell. All identities are identical in this same way, because all identities are indistinguishable.

Three-dimensional granularity gives us a new picture, a picture I cannot draw because reality cannot be presented or represented: a universe of opaque bubbles floating in space, each containing more space within its surface. Our real experience—even carefully and painstakingly examined—shows us that there can be no such "thing" as an opaque point, a dimensionless piece of contrast. With equal insistence, our experience tells us that in the real universe which we inhabit there can be no such "thing" as an infinitely large, continuous, opaque plane. We are forced—but this time gradually, by the gentle pressures and persuasions of our actuality rather than by the peremptory demands of logic or by any internal need for conviction—toward the conclusive perception that any opaque surface can only be the unbroken, finite surface of an opaque, three-dimensional, singular "thing." What was formerly a circle, at the beginning of our discussion of granularity, has become a sphere: an opaque, compoundly curved and closed surface, which so long as it really exists, divides the universe into two spaces —one of which will always be inside and the other always outside that particular, *finite* surface. You are one such space-within-a-surface. I am another. Every "thing" is, too. Instead of the distinctions between contrasting sensations, we perceive the differences between "things."

The wrapping of opacity around transparency—of surface around volume—characterizes the "real thing." This wrapping produces, further, two new, unavoidable perceptual problems, two new ways in which our relationship to any "real thing" is constantly intensified (made tense):

> First, the surface of the thing can never be entirely present to us. There is always more surface on the other side of its volume, surface which must—as its

volume must—remain hidden behind the opacity of its near face. The proportion of hidden surface— surface that is being revealed in a direction away from us (perhaps to some other person) may be small (slightly less than half) or large, and even if we have seen it before may since have changed. If one inserts this instantaneous perceptual fact into a broader perception of the thing-in-time, since all things interact with their environment, we must acknowledge that there is even more surface of the thing-in-time, which although opaque (and therefore visible), we have not seen and will not see. The better we get to know a person, for example, and the more of his behavior we are exposed to, all the more of his behavior we become aware exists elsewhere, at other times— behavior which has been or will be revealed, but *not to us,* not now, nor at any other time.

A further corollary of this first perceptual intensification of the "real thing" is the fact that two different views of the same thing (yours and mine, for example) cannot coincide. If we restrict our examination (as we must) to the opaque surface of the thing, you and I can never receive the same information from it. I can always see parts of it that are hidden from you, and vice versa. Our agreement, then, that we are perceiving the "same" object is predicated on our intensified perception that we in fact see it differently. We do not agree that it is the same *despite* the fact that it appears differently, but *because* of this fact. *Because* it appears differently to the two of us, we say it is "real," and because it is real, we say that it *is the same,* in the face of clear evidence to the contrary.[7]

---

[7] This statement contradicts the assumptions of a rationalist science which postulates experience common to all observers. Clearly, the experimental method attempts to reduce the significance of the facts I state here, and

The second intensification occurs when, in our curiosity about the transparent contents of the "real thing," we attempt to dissect it, to cut it open and find (make visible) what was hitherto hidden. If we undertake a physical dissection and actually cut the thing open, we do not find what we were looking for. Rather, we find new surface. Either we have made a new thing, with a new and different surface, or more drastically, we have made several new things instead of the one we started with. Whatever we have done, we have not "discovered" what was inside the original thing. Rather, we have made opaque what once was transparent: we have created something new.

If, in response to this observation—which is an uncertainty principle with a vengeance!—we attempt to dissect the thing in our imaginations, and from guesswork and structured thought to construct an understanding of its internal parts, asking only of ourselves that our predictions of its behavior be correct —an entirely praiseworthy effort—we should realize from the start that the better our understanding of the thing seems to work in harmony with the thing itself (i.e. we are not betrayed by its behavior), the harder it will be to "explain" (make systematically

within the language of most science their existence is both excluded and ignored. Science concerns itself with relationships of similarity, adjudged by methods of approximation, always with a "tolerance of error." The minimization of accident (unpredicted event) is the goal, the method and— predictably—the result. A concomitant result is the ignoring of all events and kinds of events which might be unpredictable. It is important to realize that unpredicted events, which constitute an enormous majority of the information we receive about the world, are neither unreal nor insignificant. One way of understanding this entire discussion is that it is an attempt to be rational about all these unpredicted events, without necessarily requiring that they become predictable. The central event with which we are concerned— our survival—cannot be predicted with certainty. Even expert assurances are not to be trusted. But—as I am trying to show—this does not mean that we cannot be rational in the face of the question, nor measure our thoughts.

opaque) that understanding to somebody else. In addition, we should acknowledge that our understanding may be shaped by the method of imaginary dissection we employ, but is dependent for its life on our own internal transparency: our consciousness flows from our own transparent capacities. We can think thoughts that we cannot understand. These thoughts may be directed toward understanding, or they may be the surface, which we are revealing to ourselves, of an understanding which we already have. Only to the extent that the information we receive from the thing across the space between it and us plunges into and reverberates freely within our internal transparency do we understand its reality.

Nothing can have any mutual reality for us except as it exists in and passes through the space between us, and so is necessarily intensified. Whether or not that exterior space is actually the interior of some other enclosing opaque surface we cannot tell, but I shall continue to call it "exterior." Within the range of our experience, all space is either interior or exterior. Further, by the postulates of granularity, these spaces alternate at every opaque surface. That is, any opaque surface has exterior space on one side of it and interior space on the other. Considered totally—by its complete enclosure—or partially—by its curvature, which distinguishes a centrality—every opaque surface is asymmetric toward the space on either side. One side faces inward, the other outward. Therefore, starting with the demands of our identity, we are first forced to accept the reality of an exterior space outside it; next, by the nonsymmetry of the relationship between our own interior space and that exterior space, via our sensations, we are further forced to the conclusion that other surfaces are nonsymmetrical in the same way, and that each of us as a "thing" inhabits a universe together with other "things" each of which also has interior identity, albeit the same kind of elusive identity which we possess (or are possessed by). Identity being what it is, we cannot distinguish between identities. Therefore, at the same time that we exercise our own identity, we exercise theirs, and vice versa. The exchange is instantaneous and complete. As we are granular, as we recognize our granularity and demonstrate the qualities of granularity, we bestow actuality on ourselves and others at the same time. The third dimension, the invisible spear of transparency, transfixes us all. The instant we present our opacity to each other, we begin to communicate and have mutual meaning: there is no way to prevent it.

By way of reminder, let me mention that there is, after all, much that can be said against what I am saying here. The solipsist—the person who logically demonstrates that, even in the midst of his demonstration, he may be talking to himself or to an illusion he has manufactured—cannot logically be budged. When we imagine the universe, we have no way of establishing at the same time that that act of imagination —which we normally assume to occur inside us—is not actually happening outside us, or that the "real world," which we normally consider to be located outside us, is not "really" inside us—it cannot rationally be denied that our experiences of reality occurs inside us. Indeed, if you didn't in some way assume the equivalence of your imagination of the world and the world, it would be difficult to act—and probably impossible to think. The critical issue is whether, although you make one thorough set of imaginary assumptions at a time in response to the world, you are willing and able to make another set at another time in response to a different world. In all its intellectual purity, the solipsist's position loses its importance in the face of this issue: so long as a response is made, and the new interchange is successful (i.e. the respondent survives), it does not matter at all whether

we call the world he is responding to "real" or "imaginary,"
"internal" or "external."

I don't really want to take on the solipsist. All I want to
point out is that once we have begun to isolate the qualities
of opacity—as I have—and have postulated transparency on
the basis that opacity makes no sense to us without it, we
must go on and postulate that every opaque surface has two
sides, and that they are different. The last postulate we are
only verging on: that by our individual, isolated assumption
of our own identity, within the opaque surface of our sensations, we can assume the same kind of asymmetry about others, and that it is the difference between inside and outside
that we most compellingly share. Not only can I not "prove
the truth" of these postulates, but I have shown, in their
own terms, why proof is impossible. But if we accept them,
we have new and interesting problems of relationship, so interesting that they take the excitement out of the solipsist's
hypothesis. We shall just tuck him under our arm and carry
on. Certainly my description of alienated isolation is enough
to gag him.

Let that suffice on finiteness and granularity for the time
being. I will return to the idea in different form.

6. In reference to communication, it seems clear that it is
transparency which, with its total lack of resistance, its un-
changing character and universal dependability, its gift of capacity in utter, nondiscriminating freedom, becomes easily
understood as the source of our experience of identity-
across-a-distance. When we trust communication, our trust is
based on transparency. We can see this in two new ways:
first, that via transparency you and I perceive the contrasts
on the surface of an opaque piece of existence outside us
both, and the existence of that contrast is what you and I
can agree on most absolutely, with the least dispute—we are,
in fact, *compelled* to agree that different things are different
(piccolo and tuba shake us to the center by their contrast, as

do azure and orange); second, since we have no way of distinguishing between our experience of internal and external transparency (an inability which is as much a result of our isolation as it is a cause of our feelings of alienation), we have no rational basis on which to distinguish what is internal to my experience and what is internal to yours. That is, the two remain hidden from each other, and *because* of this (not despite it!) we can speak to each other with hope of being understood. Communication is based more on ignorance than on knowledge. We dare make the attempt not because we can be sure of success but because we cannot be sure of failure, even after repeated rebuffs. This fact alone is enough to explain why schools, in their preoccupation with demonstrated success and failure, often teach us not to communicate. Academic activity concentrates on characteristics of the surface—behavior, skills, and demonstrable "knowledge"—and ignores what is hidden. This is not to say that a teacher can pay attention to what is hidden within his students in the same way that he can pay attention to their overt performance; nor do I mean to say that his job is to help "bring out" what is hidden within. On the other hand, he can ignore the existence of the universe of hiddens, and so imply that no such universe exists. Many teachers do. Yet that hidden universe, which I am here calling transparency, is an essential condition and ingredient of communication. A teacher's preoccupation with what is revealed and his impatience for results may suppress much that is genuine in a student.

Opacity, on the other hand, we share only because of transparency. What is opaque is itself, unsharable. By itself, opacity is not informative, it is simply information. What is opaque is, in every respect, the opposite of the transparency which allows us to perceive it. It is always diverse, accidental, and unique. Our peripheral nervous system is constructed to detect this uniqueness *and to amplify it,* a fact

which begins to explain our ability to respond strongly to
even very faint signals, seen over great distances or heard
echoing over long years. The contrasts and accidents which
form the opaque surface of a cave painting vibrate through
the same transparency which held its originator 250,000
years before, and which holds us here, now, in its spell. We
do not need a teacher's prattle or an expensive education to
lead us toward a response to this ancient insight and craft,
although it helps to have a certain sense of wonder that the
air has not since solidified, nor the human race gone blind.

It would be easy for you to understand what I have just
said about transparency and opacity as implying that communication is easy. I do mean to say that there are ways in
which we unnecessarily confuse ourselves, or let ourselves be
confused. There are even people whose clear intention is to
deceive us about ourselves, and to create the illusion of difficulty where none exists—except in the minds of those who
are deceived. On the other hand, I would be irresponsible if
I didn't try to convey the *real* difficulties involved in attempts to combine the transparent and the opaque in any
finite act of communication. It is all very well for me
blithely to remark the connection between transparency and
"identity-across-a-distance," but remarking it does not make
it happen here and now between you and me: you have to
start, here and now, with the words on this page—which can
give you, to begin with, only opacity, only distinctions, only
contrasts between this and that word, this and that para-
graph, this and that reference to reality. I remind you of the
rational perspective which allowed me with confidence to say
that the internal *physical* states of two people cannot be the
same at any time or over any period of time (pp. 24–26), so
that "identity-across-a-distance" refers to something that is
critically *not* physical, yet within the terms of this discussion, *is real*. Only by trusting it as real *but partial* can you
trust your understanding. It is equally casual of me to re-

mark that on distinctions and contrasts you and I are most clearly compelled to agree: that agreement, by itself, cannot possibly mean that you and I understand each other. Both my attempt to communicate my understanding and your attempt to understand it are hard work.

7. The relationship between opacity and transparency, the complementarity of their qualities, and their minute and general connection to the "physical" universe perceived as their perpendicularity are so basic that they generate many important, analogous relationships. It is a strong temptation to see, in the opaque-transparent relationship, something so fundamental as to provide a valid basis for a theory of being —a temptation which I have given up resisting. As can be seen from the following arrangement of references, the range of implication is large. The possibility—no, the *probability* that communication is a subfunction of being is large. That doesn't really say it clearly, since being and communication are simultaneous occurrences. I am suggesting that although we can learn much about being from communication, we can learn much more about communication from being. We can, after all, say many things that have little or no communicative meaning, but even the smallest segment of being has infinite potential meaning. The necessities and intentions of being are more powerful than those of any communicative act.

8. As I have used them throughout this text, the words "actual," "real," "being," and "total experience" should be understood in this context: that at all times there is a transparency within us, an opacity at our surface, a transparency outside that surface, an opacity at the surface of all else, and an obscure transparency within all else. The context of any one of these pieces is, at any time, all the rest, and although they thereby should be considered to be coexistent—without remission or alternative—each also remains at all times distinct.

TRANSPARENCY : OPACITY	TRANSPARENCY : OPACITY
Unseen : Seen	Theory : Data
Unsensed : Sensed	Time : Event
Hiddenness : Revelation	History : Historical fact
Continuity : Discontinuity	Import : Information
Connection : Separation	Content : Form
Identity : Distinction	Meaning : Sign (signal)
Space : Surface	Energy : Material surface
Volume : Surface	Will : Action
No-change : Change	Stability : Variety
Function : Form	Flexibility : Rigidity
Intention : Action	

As these distinctions are maintained, we survive.

Or, as we maintain this actuality we maintain our own actuality. The actuality of our survival will embody the actuality of our perceptions, the actuality of our communications, the actuality of our feelings, and the actuality of our thoughts. And in all these, the idea of actuality is an important aid.

9. Finally, although there are many other human problems that can profitably be discussed in terms of transparency, opacity, and their relationship, right here, now —perhaps illogically—I would like to point out the connection between them and the old problem of freedom and constraint.

Freedom first. I have already doled out a big dose of freedom in discussing the infinite qualities of transparency and opacity. Each in its own way is a constantly present, inexhaustible bootstrap. One or the other can be a source of release from internal tension, of protection from external restriction. Release can be gained by instant mental transport or by clambering up the painstaking handholds of existence; protection can be achieved, as in judo, by disappearing (via identification) into the motion of the attacker, or by the more ordinary fabrication of an opaque, enigmatic wall of behavior, decorated with the crenellations of threat. Transparency contributes to our lives the notion of no restraint, of infinite space and time—that all is possible, and there is no hurry about it. Opacity contributes the actuality of number, the leverage of difference, and the immediacy, urgency, unexpectedness—and priceless value—of the absolutely new. Together, transparency provides the space into which the opaque, violent colors of a revolutionary perception explode.

In balance to this it is fair to see that both transparency and opacity have limitations. Outside of those I am too blind to see, there are the ones they clearly give each other. For example, transparency can never be confronted. It always escapes observation. Even our consciousness of it is something else besides: to think of it is to lie about it to oneself; to speak of it is to lie to whomever hears you. Transparency is inarticulate, mute, a shadow of a shadow of a shadow. You can never use it, it is never an instrument, and therefore cannot give you a "way to freedom." No, transparency you always already have, the freedom that preceded you: in your concrete being, you are always limited compared to it. If you find it, the act is no discovery but more a remembrance, a revitalization of that space into which you were born. It is well to remember that at that moment of maximum freedom, you were never more powerless.

As a surface which changes all that impinges on it and thereby brings it to an end, opacity seems to be equivalent to limitation. Opacity and constraint are identical. Yet opacity is itself unrestrained: since it is comprised only of contrast it can only move forward and leave behind. So it is forever barred from making sense or providing cohesion to the universe. Its insufficiency here is closely related to its concreteness: each opaque field is unique, nonsensical, and unrelated to any other. One may look to opacity to find freedom, but alone it will make no sense and satisfy no urges because it is entirely without repose. Its limitation has no limits.

It is only when combined that opacity and transparency can begin to work. Each overcomes the limitations of the other, but in so doing loses—in a way beyond easy explanation—its extreme freedom. As we combine them in our growth, freedom becomes finite and vulnerable both to work and to bad luck.

So one muses. But we are more than minds just as we are more than emotions. At our fullest moments, when we feel that our thoughts are perfectly in tune with reality, and our thoughts confirm those feelings, how do we experience opacity and transparency? Separately each is an enemy or antithesis of life, although we feel a pull toward each. Opacity defines the pole of our absurdity and the absurdity of our existence: all is separate, all is nonsense, nothing can have meaning because meaning itself has none. "Our nada who are in nada, nada be thy name." Pointed in this direction, one is in the proper frame of mind to play Russian roulette —or any of the other more sophisticated and socialized ways we have to toy with death. Transparency defines a different kind of nothingness, one which fills "the abyss's void with emptiness." From it comes the urge, for example, to submerge the aches and agonies of old age in the pure flow of time: if one could simply sink beneath the water and float with it back out to sea, one would be participating in being. Death achieved in this way would be free, even, of guilt.

So long as we are alive we are held away from either pole of nothingness: we are held to be something. As something we walk between absurdity and the abyss. On this middle ground, where two kinds of nothing meet, where the always-hidden meets the only-revealed, between these two empty horizons, something rises up here which both gives us life and demands that we live. In these hills we find joy.

This is the normal experience: when time passes, even a tiny bit of time, something new is revealed which suggests that it hides something else. The more clearly and sharply drawn are our sensations of this newness and the more rapidly they rain on us, the more they insist that they are significant. And the more obscure, at that moment, their significance. At one and the same time we are enlivened by a fresh and energetic desire to understand this newness, and know that it will take a long time to do so—perhaps longer than our lives. Life is undeniably worth living, and livable in its own terms.

In these moments, the opaque and the transparent have combined without becoming confused. These are the peak conditions of life. Under these conditions of clarity, what is transparent is divided by the opaque into three: what is within each of us, what is between us, and what is within all else. At the same time, the opaque is distilled from the transparent into two: our sensations and the fresh-cut surface of the universe. *Despite* these divisions (I say that to warn your mind) and *because* of them (I say that to remind your heart), you and the universe are unified and significant to each other—unified by the transparent and made significant by the opaque. Beside this actuality, the idea or ideal of the beautiful or the good is a shadow in the mind.

For the moment here I am struggling for truth. The thoughts twist and turn with reverberations near and far, old and new. They always try to escape, to move on. Trying to hold them, I stare out the window. The sun is shining in and onto the desk. Amid the crisscrossed shadow lines of mullions and muntins, the glass lets through bright sun-patches which fold over the clutter of books and papers and magazines. Toward the edge of one clear rectangle of light there is a black spot of shadow as if somewhere on the window pane were a one-inch circle of black paper. As I locate the source of this strange shadow, I see that it is merely a small dimple in the glass. The transparent material is mis-shapen there, and to my squinting, squeezes and obscures a spot on the landscape beyond. Just by bending some of the light rays, this transparent glass dimple has become totally opaque, even to the rays of the sun.

I know, even as I struggle to say something true, that I have many more wrinkles than this pane of glass and that, even as I make these words try to be "clear," what has become unhidden here is different from what I mean. And so I stop, abruptly. My intention has existed, and such is the result so far.

ASSEMBLY *talk by a guest speaker, perhaps in April, maybe May:*

"Politics," they say, "is the art of the possible." By which they mean to say that it's all very well for those people without power to dream, but there are limits. Not everything is possible, so be content. Politics is the best we can do, at least with these particular people in power.

Now of all the meaningless statements I have heard, that one contains the most meaninglessness, or at least the most misleadingness. I am no politician—nothing is more distasteful to me than the thought of being beholden for my entire life and living to a few million scratches on paper, backed by a few million erroneous opinions. (I wouldn't mind being a legislator, though.) As I say, I'm not a politician, but I know a good deal about the "art of the possible." *Art* is the art of the possible. I say that because from time to time I try to be an artist, and it is hard. Finding out what is possible is the beans and mush of art, its lifeblood, its epitome. Art is ninety-five per cent trying things out. The other five per cent is actually doing it, which means a lot of throwing away. Sure, there are a lot of compromises involved be-

tween wish and fulfillment, between ambition and public response. That's where some of the art comes in, to
compromise without seeming to. At times it is indistinguishable from frustration, or even failure. A few people
manage to match dream and deed so that maybe no compromise seems suffered—but we can't tell. Maybe they just have
a flippant lip or a hardened heart. Maybe they are just hiding.

Of course there are those of you who are neither politicians nor artists: you may have other ideas. Perhaps *cooking*
is the art of the possible? Or *eating? Engineering? Education?* Let's compromise on *living.* How's that? "Living is the
art of the possible." You notice that the politician (along
with his cynical followers) has lost his basic claim here, while
the artist still retains a foothold in the statement. ("Art may
not be a living, but certainly living is an art," they say.)

"Living is the art of the possible." Well well.

But let me go back a bit. The statement *I* like best is, "Art
is the art of the possible." There is an admirable circularity
there, a kind of teasing, a flirting with meaning. Maybe
something is being said. If *art* is *the art of the possible,* then
the art of the possible is *the art of the art of the possible.*
And our original statement becomes—at this temporary
stopping point in our logic—"Art is the art of the art of the
art of the possible." And so forth. As we progress further, we
end up still with only one "possible" and hundreds of multi-
plying "arts," which is as it should be. The statement begins
to take on a certain mathematical, not to say arithmetical, el-
egance (which always tends to legitimize statements, whatever they mean), and to leave our first, more primitive forms
of the statement behind in the dust. This one has more
meaning. It is longer. And with due respect, the others can
now be shortened to "politics is an art," "living is an art,"
"education is an art," etc. As these newly lit statements begin
to shine like beacons in the darkness of our lives, and we

begin to hope that meaninglessness has finally met its match, just remember who told you.

As for me, the next time somebody tells me, with wisdom lurking in his eye, that politics is the art of the possible, I shall tell him sternly, "I am much more interested in the art of the impossible." That will get him in his gauntlet!

4 The best communication is an exchange of gifts; the skills involved are those of offering and receiving; the values involved are generosity and gratitude.

These statements have a moral ring. I intend them to, but not immediately. Let me try to give them some substance before you say either "yes, yes" or "not at all."

The best communication is an exchange of gifts:

"Best communication" needs a context before it will mean much, a context of communication which is less than best. Let me draw two pictures, two images of two different kinds of communication, two common but contrasting ways of seeing our communicative acts, which are less than best.

The first (figure 4) could be called straight-line or centrifugal radiation. In this category are all those particles of information and forms of energy that any organism—anything—emits freely, constantly, "accidentally," simply because it exists: modulations of light, heat, noise, etc., which have nothing directly or purposefully to do with its survival (that we know of) and which, in effect, are not intentional. Also include all responses by the organism that are essentially reflexive: automatic, consistent, highly predictable, and as each organism remains unconscious of them, beneath its concern or control. Finally, include those actions which may have a communicative purpose or intention, but of which the destination or recipient is either unknown, unknowable, or a matter the initiating organism chooses not to know. Desperate cries for help when we have no idea they will be heard; nondiscriminatory dissemination of information via publication or broadcast where there is no specific intent to affect a particular person; the blind crying of an angry infant; an impersonal governmental edict or law; the billboard on a country barn; a bomb falling fifty thousand feet on to a company of enemy soldiers; a bomb falling fifty thousand feet on to a bus full of innocent schoolchildren; the scholarly dissertation of an obscure and unambitious scientist; the light from the sun; the nervous, caffein-induced twitch in the finger

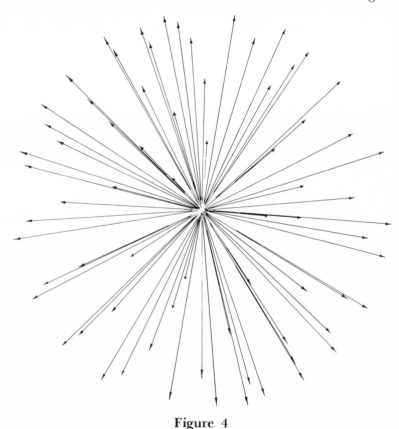

Figure 4

poised over the last red button which will blast us all into subatoms.

The assumptions and experience which will allow us to see straight-line radiation as a real form of communication are the same assumptions and experience which underlie our notions of objective science, of pure justice, of the existence of purposeless accident, and of identifiable cause and effect: that undistorted change can occur over a distance, that information exists and travels, pure and unadulterated, and, broadly speaking, that nature—if you keep your eyes open —throws no curves. It is by straight-line radiation that truth will prevail. The disciplines coming from these assumptions are rational, precise, careful, self-confident, and capable of extremes of insensitive cruelty. In the eye of the mind so shaped the universe is imagined as a collection of point-sources-and-receptors of energy, a network of interlocked pinpricks of change, an empty night-field filled with named starpoints whre things happen. Transparent space is at all times, at all points full of information that has radiated from these myriad sources of energy: if we place the properly sensitive instruments at any point, an infinite amount of opaque "true" information is immediately at our disposal. We ourselves are walking instrument packages. So effectively do we collect information that we must screen most of it out on some "rational" basis. The ultimate knowledge is statistical. Decisions are weighted averages of information. The goal is perfection of idea via approximation. The shortest distance is always straight, always single, and always selfless. You, as self, are reduced to a center-of-gravity, a point where all your communicative interactions intersect, and where any movement takes all else with it. the naiveté of this kind of idealism, combined with its mechanical practicality, has become, as you know, incredibly sophisticated in its application. Its brutality is hidden beneath the maze of a technology bought and paid for, willy-nilly, at great price—technology and its price have created our albatross of affluence.

The second image, or form, or communication (figure 5) consists entirely of feedback loops, in which every outward moving act stimulates some returning result, some gratifying, self-adjusting or self-preserving effect, even over great distances. Every motion is a reaching out toward an event at the farthest point of the arc, where the desired return is triggered. Back it comes. The effort is rewarded, and the organ-

Figure 5

ism is encouraged to try again. It does, and succeeds. In this category are those actions we call "purposeful," "useful," "ambitious," "self-indulgent," "successful," "effective," or (at times) "organized." The intent of these communicative acts is control, and the intent of the control is to establish and maintain circular patterns of interactive exchange—continuous and uninterrupted even at the "means" and "ends" points. The goal, the motivation, the method, and the reward, as they lie around this circular path, are inseparable. The perfect achievement of this kind of communicative effort is an effortlessness as easy as breathing, in which the relationship is so well-protected from accidental and other "foreign" interruptions that it is difficult if not impossible to define the borders of the organism. Its external exchanges work as smoothly as its internal ones: its symbiotic relationship with its environment is so *organic* that one wonders whether its environment is not an indistinguishable part of the organism, or the organism an indistinguishable part of its environment. Which, in fact, is the possessor, which the possessed? Examples: the mutual absorption of two lovers; an old man in the protective custody of habitual existence; eating; the fateful "chicken come home to roost" of long-forgotten origin, which may be tragic or bountiful; a child in the moments of his perfect play; the motions and mannerisms of a man on the make; a policeman controlling violence by hitting somebody on the head; a protestor protesting violence by throwing a brick; a nation "giving" aid to another in return for economic and political involvement; the addict of any sort, up to and including the one hooked on using people; the masochist who tricks somebody into hurting him; the man who dreams that he has pushed the last red button which will blast us all into subatoms and wakes up to find that he actually has.

The assumptions and experience underlying our acceptance of the reality of the feedback image also underlie such disciplines as biology, sociology, and psychology. A large body of conventional wisdom has it that all animal behavior is an efficient display of self-seeking, self-preserving, self-referring intention; that we, as animals, are incapable of sustained—or even slightly purposeful—magnanimity or altruism; that our espousal of high ideals is a rationalized mask to hide other, much less admirable motives; that each of us must obey the territorial imperative, even if the territory claimed is only within one's body; that a society is essentially a means to maximize the satisfaction of most of its members and to minimize their trespass or interference; and that this "social" need is so great as to define a true norm—a conservative, stable state of social existence toward which all people, even in conflict, fall back. The disciplines of understanding this kind of communication are full of suspicion and guesswork, doubt and double-dealing, and are capable of extremes of cynical cruelty and social manipulation. As "instrument packages" walking through this kind of universe, we are forced to confront the fact that there are impenetrable barriers to certain kinds of information, and that even though there are infinite quantities of information to sift and measure, there is, beyond this amount, an even greater quantity of information which will never be realized by us. Once it has turned opaque, information cannot be freed in its original power. To the mind so shaped by these images of suspicion and sacrifice, the universe is seen as a dense network of greedy organisms whose every act, bent by the magnetism and gravity of selfness, returns to each what it can efficiently wrest from the others and our common, stingy surroundings. The ultimate knowledge is pessimistic. Decisions are attempts to beat the game. The goal is efficient satisfaction. All lines are curved and eventually return to themselves, suggesting both orderliness and futility. We are left with a sense of both as we recognize ourselves in this picture.

These images give us polar contrasts: between the pattern

of paths by which each describes the shape of our intention; between their conceptual contexts (the "possible universe" each suggests); between the kinds of knowledge and ideas of truth each implies; between the inescapable suggestions each makes about what we are and can do; and particularly between the kinds of relationships we can feel toward each other. Their polarity reminds us of the polarity between transparency and opacity. Is the relationship between straight-line and feedback communication the same as the relationship between transparency and opacity? If we catch a forward pass from that prior discussion we find in our hands not one other example of their contrast to add to our list (p. 111), but two contrasting examples of how they combine.

In the straight-line image of radiation, the presumed relationship between transparency and opacity is very similar to our original description: their difference is abstract and absolute, their relationship is nonspecific—a matter of general "fact" rather than of our desire, and therefore analogous to the relationship between two adjacent parts of an opaque field. The difference between opacity and transparency is noted but not put to use. If the straight-line image is taken as complete, if we (and all other "objects") are regarded as point centers of energy exchange, then there is no room within us and no place outside us for either intention or an orderly relationship between understanding and the universe. The only possible relationship could be on a one-to-one basis, each segment of the universe, each bit of information matched to a segment or bit of understanding. Understanding could earn the right of legitimacy only by becoming as exposed as the rest of the universe—only by becoming opaque. Where before the existence of understanding we had one opaque universe, now we would have two: our understanding would become something more to understand, and then so would that next understanding. Explanation piles on explanation, in a tedious pursuit of instant truth. The hiddenness of transparency is denied (and apparently feared). Our statistical compromises are attempts to whitewash the absurdity implicit in the image—*our* absurdity, I mean.

In the feedback image we reintroduce, but in a new way, the idea of granularity: at some radius from the center of the organism there is a sphere which contains all its interactions, because all its significant emanations return to it. This sphere defines a threshold beyond the self does not extend.[8] In showing this limitation, the feedback image suggests within this boundary a hiddenness, a withinness, a withdrawal of the organism from all others into its finiteness. Nothing escapes from within its "sphere of influence," and so, from outside it, nothing of its workings can be seen, while once within it, one becomes part of it: one shares its identity. With the feedback image, all space becomes a space of purpose, finitely divided into bubbles of self-reference between which ignorant toleration is the only compromise possible, and existence is comprised mainly of competition, stabilized by selfishness. Identity has, in the feedback image, become a "self." "Self-consciousness" takes charge of ourselves. But as you become conscious of your consciousness, and think about thought, the new possibility of thinking about that new thought comes into being, and then further, you can think about *that* thought, and become conscious that you are conscious of consciousness. So begins an endless circular chase into internal transparency by which you are forced to admit that you cannot know the difference between knowledge and the act of knowing.

Two extremes, two kinds of consistency, two kinds of absurdity. As in the case of transparency and opacity, can we combine them, can we somehow turn the fallings-away of each to good account? Can we make a better guess about the

[8] We ignore the possibility that this sphere is infinitely large; imagined, the possibility hints at the solipsist's image of self and universe identified.

paths of our communicative acts as we send them into the
transparency around us? Yes, at least, we sometimes do, and
our doing precedes any analysis. Their combined images are
not just an overlay (figure 6). Their graphic synthesis is a
combination of circularity and straight line: the creation of
new, separate, self-referring objects or "grains of being"
which are moving outward from the source. The communicative message we see as a "thing" rather than only a cry for
help in a vacuum or an attempt to control other organisms.
The message has been invested with a life of its own and
sent on its way. It has been offered. *It has become a gift.*

Suddenly the communicative act assumes an entirely dif-

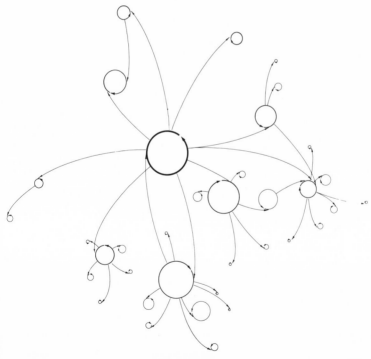

Figure 6

ferent significance, new possibilities of freedom. Seen in this
way it can lead us away from both absurdity and futility—if
we let it. Even the smallest flicker of message assumes a new
importance if we treat it as a new resident of the universe,
an inhabitant of reality with equal rights—rather than the
accidental gleam from another tiny, buffeted space-dweller
in hugeness, or, more cynically, his attempt to capture us to
his purposes and hold us in his orbit. The message becomes
part of the intermediate, granular reality which shares, with
each of us, both extreme possibilities of communication.
From the straight-line, radiant image it assumes the characteristics of independence, of motion-across-a-distance, of
spontaneous effect, of risk-taking and accident, of immediacy, of susceptibility to cool and critical examination, of
ruthlessness, and of the possibility of infinitely spreading result. From the feedback image it assumes the characteristics
of curvature, of centeredness, of self-reference, of intention,
of doubleness, (even duplicity—*timeo Danaos*), of hiddenness, of organic interchange with its surroundings, of inter-
dependency, of personal value, and the capability of being
forgotten or even unnoticed.

As a newly created piece of the world, the communicated
gift becomes more than its intention: it becomes public, for
example, independent of its source or destination, and vulnerable to destruction, responsive to preservation. Perhaps
most important is what this change does to us. If we must
treat our intermediate gifts as we treat each other—as things
with *content,* as possessing a hidden quantity of permanent
value from which an investment of time will derive permanent reward—then our relationship *to each other* changes
drastically. Not until we treat what we say to and do with
each other as having an independent content does our relationship become more than a combination of accident and
mutual usefulness. As we face each other and are engaged,
this is not an easy perception to achieve, nor does it feel, at

all times, natural. Most important, it raises between us the problems of *meaning,* of *misunderstanding,* of *sophistication,* and of *value.* In other words, when we see our communication as an exchange of gifts, our experience of any actual piece of interchange includes some strongly felt questions:

> What is the relationship between the tangible "wrapping" of this gift and its hidden content? What *is* its hidden content? How do I experience it? How did its originator experience it? What is the relationship between his and my experience? How does that relate to his intent? To my satisfaction?
>
> How do I know whether I can trust my experience of the content of the gift, even when I feel sure of it? Isn't it likely that if what you or I say *is* independent of us in some ways, we misunderstand each other most of the time? How can we know if we don't, even when we think not?
>
> Doesn't the independence of our mutually offered gifts demand, then, a constant checking and rechecking of what they are or were? A constant increase in our sensitivity? An increased consideration of alternate possibilities of meaning and mutual interpretation? Doesn't our relationship become overly complicated? Does this complication ever stop? How can we achieve simplicity without being stupid?
>
> Are all gifts equally well given? Aren't some more valuable than others? Don't some masquerade as gifts but are really attempts to manipulate? How do I distinguish between them? How do I know my judgment is trustworthy?

As these newly created questions begin to occur, remember that they cannot be "answered"; *they exist only as the context of our mutual actions.* They are the space we cross when we speak to each other. Our intentions give us motion, our actions carry us across, but the space itself never disappears. In fact, at times it seems as though our mutual actions have life *only* because they breathe the air between us: the gift absorbs much of its value from the space it crosses to reach us.

The skills involved are those of offering and accepting: These skills are self-taught.

Whether or not you learn them is up to you.

I say this because accepting is a form of giving: most people must exert themselves to take advice, for example, or to learn from the words of another—even well-intentioned words. Sermons accomplish little. For some reason we trust our own daily experience more than the brief needlings of an expert. The teacher-preacher may raise questions about what we believe, but it is unlikely he can persuade us to share his beliefs.

If we are going to learn about giving, it will happen in our daily doings with people. In these circumstances, communication is homemade and makeshift: if it is easy, it is old; if it is new, it is awkward. But to speak of giving is to speak of newness. We might as well face that fact and accept that daily offering is likely to be awkward. To ridicule awkwardness is to kill generosity along with the gift, for in awkward words often lies new truth, even poetry. Toward each other we are perfectly capable of maintaining an openness and readiness to appreciate the new as it tries to find its way into the light. If we laugh, let it be in delight.

The awkwardness of daily generosity has alternatives, though. We do not have to commit ourselves immediately into the open, nor rush ahead stumbling and grabbing for support here and there. We can go slowly and make preparations. In solitude we can anticipate and try things out, and the results need not be elaborate, although they may be called "art." Face-to-face conversation, if relaxed, can be careful, too. Beyond that, there are many forms of communication, many kinds of gifts, which to bring into being require tremendous amounts of time, of person, of sensitivity, and of control. Before it can be offered, the gift must be made. Before it can be made, it must be intended. Before it can be intended, it must be dreamt. And before it can be dreamt, there must be a time of dreaming.

Dreaming time is squandered. It is time spent so recklessly that if it were ever considered to be money, the dreamer must be the world's richest man. Dreaming time is free, without charge, although it is the source of all real value to our lives. Any child knows that the sole purpose of all the trappings of our existence, all the hustle, all the necessities of eating and maintaining the peace are solely to enable us to dream, to let us begin to create new being. All else is merely circumstantial, instrumental, or dependent to the dream. Dreaming time is enormous, unlimited, and must be treated with appropriate respect and absolute immunity, for it is the mother of all giving. The dream is the child fathered by experience on dreaming time: in that womb, imagination recapitulates creation. In the stirrings of anticipation the dream assumes an intention. Gradually we lend our wider skills—all that we have—and shape the intention into a making. Our making bursts into being. Then— perhaps without much additional effort—the gift can be offered.

The metamorphosis from dream into being is accompanied by several other changes: from dream time to actual time; from expansive, unrooted imagination to effort limited by skills and circumstance; from our broadest humanity to our idiosyncratic person; from openness to all sensation to acceptance and pursuit of restriction, selection, and discard; from a sense of identity with meaning to a motion away from it into hiding and guessing; from a floating in all-time to an urgency to get the job done, the gift made and given; from all-encompassing generosity and good will to a particular act of giving this gift to this person at this time. Once given, no backward look.

These changes ring on the capacities of the whole person, whose wholeness has been allowed, who has not ignored his own impulses to be whole, to reach into the farthest nooks and around the farthest corners of his being, not to enforce a singleness on his self, but to find the variety which his identity holds. Part of this wholeness is his ability and willingness to be a "different person" at different stages in the process of giving. The person wholly involved in dreaming is a different organism from the person wholly involved in making. It takes more than skill to learn how to change from one to the other, as one must do in a generous stance toward the world: it takes a lack of fear or compulsion about what one is, and a willingness to find out. If one is truly dreaming, making the dream actual cannot be dreamt, and when the time for making comes, it is a harsh awakening. To expect otherwise is simply to increase the pain.

Giving requires discipline. As the gift begins to coalesce, to shrink into actuality, to change from wish to an independent and vulnerable being, we (the givers) must learn to ignore our desires, to discard fragments of ourselves, to open ourselves to rebuff, to criticism, or—the most appalling—to lack of any response. As we offer this new thing no longer a dream, it begins to draw away from us and to hide its meaning even from us who made it. Even what was not given, was never intended, becomes part of the gift. In this realignment of reality, the new existence assumes shape, and becomes formal. Not only does it take on an opaque surface, but it begins to inhabit its own limited volume. It has become another finite grain of actuality. With its independence come tremendous new pressures and limitations. The universe is a large, crowded place: the only way it can thank the giver (apparently) is to suffer the survival of his gift, at least until it is accepted.

To each other we can, of course, say our thanks, but that is a small gesture compared to our accepting each other's gifts. Accepting is much more than "catching babies," as hardened obstetrical interns call their job. In some ways accepting is the reverse of offering: starting with the form of the gift, we pass through an appreciation of its details and variations to an enlarged sense of personal investment (which cannot help but be both ours and the giver's). Once we accept the reality of the gift, we can take it all the way into the life and time where the truth is most for us: we can accept it into our dreaming. Because we have received the gift, our truth has changed. The truth I give is trusted because I have dreamt it and it can make new dreams.

If we stop and examine our acceptance, we find that it is more active than the word implies. A gift does not, itself, ever become something different by our accepting it. It does not relapse into dream. The gift remains—so long as it is alive—a fresh source of newness. Our choice to let it reinvade our inner selves is always renewable. This choice is, like offering, an act of generosity, but one which is unseen: no overt gift results, yet accepting is an act of giving. Giving remains at the heart of all communication: as the gift is offered, so is its acceptance.

The values involved are generosity and gratitude:

As accepting seems to be a form of offering, so gratitude seems to be a form of generosity. If one is capable of being generous, he is capable of being grateful.

Nobody can be persuaded to be generous. Somebody persuaded to give is not really offering, no more than the person persuaded to receive is really accepting. But before you choose to become generous—if you do—it helps to know that it is possible. Even more, it helps to know the terms in which it is possible.

We can give to each other *because* we are alone. We do

not overcome solitude by giving. Rather, we acknowledge it and suggest that it can be endured and even, at moments, acutely enjoyed. To find that you are able to be freely generous is one of the greatest pleasures existence grants you—a pleasure which is not reached by ambition nor rewarded with pride. You may think that my gradual approach to this central issue between us (which lies between all people at all times) has been too roundabout, too indirect. Given what I am trying to say, what else could I do? I mention our limitations not in order that we do less for each other, but that we do not lay ourselves and others open to a pain amplified by its unexpectedness.

I bring forward, finally, the main points between you and me:

Because we are actually separate, we are independent.

Because we are independent, we communicate neither to control nor to consume each other.

Our communication consists of offering into and accepting across the distance between us, each from his privacy.

Because that distance cannot be crossed by understanding, nor can we make that distance disappear, our communication consists of offering and accepting gifts.

These gifts are actual, as we are, and are therefore distant from us—with all the aspects of distance that I have described.

Because of transparency, the gift can move between us, but its movement cannot be stopped.

Because of its opacity, the gift is revealed and hides what it contains.

Because of the two together, the gift is actual and assumes both life and ambiguity.

Finally, because to make a gift and to accept a gift require all our capacities—and this with no guarantee of success—the primary requirement for communication is generosity.

So. We give because we give. We give in order to give. We do not give what we have been given. In giving, we make new being. We give because our wholeness has become large. We give because we have become generous.

FIVE fireflies
Greendimly dashdotting

Here we are
Here we are

To whom?

5 Uncles and Earthquakes

I DON'T know whether it is simply a biological re-verberation across two time zones, or something more profound—a reaching backward to those early summer mornings when my alarm was the brief rumble of logs as my father dumped them on the living-room hearth, and I would get up in the cold, numb with sleep, and go in just to smell the new smoke as it wisped and crept from the logs across the chilly floor before the draft got going, and wake slowly as the tongues of flame flickered and focused with my eyes. At any rate, I have wakened, here in California, at three-fifteen a.m., thirty years later, in a mood of alert reverie which reminds me of that time, and in so doing, of the prices I have paid since—of the social smoke and fog of convention, which in their misty mythicality, have formed solid ghosts in my

135

mind. Perhaps that slow, early awakening was preparation for the later invasion. By beating the clock here and now, I anticipate my habitual social thought and so can be selective toward it when it arrives with the sun, and give it the resistance it deserves.

As I say, maybe I felt a twinge of more recent habit and am simply waking up with New England. If so, that social sympathy leaves me alone, here, and I can turn the habit to unexpected use. For a few hours, this house on the Point Reyes Peninsula—which has been called because of its local geological precedence "an island in time"—can be an important refuge. I have a space in which to think special thoughts about the rest of the world. In moments like these one can feel equal to any society, and able to give advice: for the fact that society disappears utterly when people sleep demonstrates beyond the shadow of a doubt that society is only a waking dream, a habit of thought which obeys only the laws of the mind. Society is stubborn and tough to newness, yet strangely mutable, subject to fits of madness, but above all else—of this we are reminded by its nightly dying—it is mortal. We can, in simple honesty, stare even the greatest of world powers in the eye of its mundane assumptions and say, "I may well outlive and outlast you."

It is difficult to realize that during the seven months since we came here this entire peninsula—a wide isosceles triangle which rests its twenty-nine-mile earth-and-water base on the mainland, right along the San Andreas Fault, and pushes its altitude southwest twelve miles into the Pacific—has moved north by west slightly more than an inch with respect to the rest of the country. Along the fault line, fifty miles deep, rocks are actually bending to accommodate this movement. At some time, sooner or later, along some line of fracture the stress will find release: the rocks will break and slide by each other, seeking new alignment, new equilibrium. And then start bending again. It will happen within a minute as it did in 1906. While the stone underpinnings of the entire land-scape rethink their position, we humans on the surface, like flies displaced by the shiver of a horse's skin, will experience another earthquake, buzz awhile, and resettle.

I thought it had come, two Saturdays ago. Sue and I were upstairs in the study when the house trembled. Windows rattled intently, the floor shook, and our nerves assumed the worst. We both were on our feet immediately, and as I ran downstairs, another shock came. Our sons were on the beach, but my sister's two sons were out on the porch, where they had been playing a guitar and a dulcimer, singing softly. They had stopped, and I said, "Did you feel something?" I was wondering why Sue didn't come down.

"Yeah, sort of," said Ethan, the elder.

"We didn't know what it was," said Andy. Both were, like me, newcomers to California, but Andy had been here only two days.

"I was thinking it was an earthquake," I said, visualizing the house as a mass of rubble. I had a picture of digging out my manuscript and the typewriter, and had a flash-feeling that if only I could get them both down to the car I could endure any catastrophe. Meanwhile, I couldn't understand why Ethan and Andy remained so calm.

"I was reading about earthquakes." I said. "They say there are foreshocks and aftershocks—before and after the big one. Maybe those were foreshocks."

"Oh?" They joked a bit about it, but as we chatted, and I waited for the "big one," I realized, suddenly, that to them the idea of an earthquake was different from mine. They were interested in the idea of a new experience, and didn't grasp the possibility that the entire deck we were standing on might suddenly, with a sideways jolt, splinter, buckle, and fall with the house folding down the hill over it. I walked over to the steps and waited, ready to run down, as we talked.

Their calm was more functional than my fear. There were no further shocks, nor any reports of tremors on the evening news.

The next day, the plan had been for Sue and our boys to drive with Ethan and Andy up to a state park, inland from the Peninsula, to walk with them for a day, and then to drive back, leaving my nephews to hike over to the shore and back home along the beach, taking a couple more days. But when Sunday morning came, our boys—who were facing Monday-morning school—decided they would prefer to loaf, and Sue didn't feel well, so I said I'd take Ethan and Andy up, and then maybe I would drive over to the Point Reyes Seashore Headquarters and walk around their "Earthquake Trail," a short hike, to see some traces of the 1906 earthquake, and wondered if any of my children wanted to come with me. But nobody did, so I would go alone.

Along about eleven, after Ethan and Andy had spent two hours getting their food together and deciding what clothes to take and borrowing utensils and trading sleeping bags (ours were lighter), the three of us loaded their two packs and a dried spaghetti dinner into the back of the bus and drove up to Olema. The two boys were large and quiet. Just the size of their bodies beside the not-so-old image of their infancy made me shy. Who knows how their minds work by comparison? Do they now have thoughts as big as their thumbs have grown? And, for some reason, they are shy with me—or at least quiet. I can remember being so quiet myself, and think there's probably little I can do to break its sources into the open. Besides, I respect it.

Ethan pointed to a hill on the left. "Look, Andy, at that place where the trees thin below the line of the hill's silhouette. It looks like there's a hole right through the hill, as if the hill were as thin as paper. Or as if the sky you can see through there has been painted on the front of the hill.

Strange!" Andy looked and said nothing.

At Olema I asked whether they wanted to drop by the Seashore Headquarters and reserve a campsite for the next night. "No, we'll go there tomorrow, on our way in." So we turned right onto the highway and started east into the grassy hills.

I forget the next slow, spaced series of exchange, but I do remember something about leaving the spaghetti dinner behind while they walk for a day, maybe underneath a bush. And Ethan said, maybe in the car, and I drew a blank and said maybe under a bush or behind a tree. And when, a minute later, he erupted, saying, "You mean, you're just going to *abandon* us?" with a note of overdrama in his voice, I thought it was a bit of surreal humor, hinting at a certain ambivalence in his feelings about the whole idea of camping out, so I just smiled; and it wasn't until we had reached the park, unloaded their packs, slipped the spaghetti dinner into a zippered compartment of Andy's pack—until they had hoisted on their packs, and after a backward look to me at the bottom, started up the steep hill across the road—and until I had started back to Olema that I realized, with a shock, that they had been expecting me to walk with them that day, and had planned to pick up the spaghetti dinner only when we returned to the car.

I knew why I hadn't noticed—sheer stupidity, combined with the fact that I had never intended to go. So the question took shape, if I had never intended to go, why did they think that I had? Part of that was easy: their original plan had been to walk with Sue and the boys, so just as my *not* going fulfilled my plan, their assumption that I *was* going was a continuance of their plan. And since I had never discussed their plans, and they had never discussed mine, all the time we had been riding in the same car, together, we had actually been going in different directions. They had been going on a walk with me; I was going to drop them off and drive on to the Seashore, where I wanted to walk around the Earthquake Trail.

I almost turned back, but I knew I couldn't find them. Besides, there were further subtleties to think about. I couldn't help guessing that some of the confusion came from Ethan and Andy's perceptual linking of me with the family; that in some respects, when I got into the car to drive them up, they saw "Uncle-Bob-instead-of-Aunt-Sue." I was another tree they couldn't see for the family forest. I was not only their substitute driver, I was their substitute companion as well. Their shock when they found I wasn't coming on the walk came at the betrayal of what was to them a comfortable and intimate reality, despite the fact that that reality was untrue.

This was a situation so familiar—as it is to any teacher—that I couldn't help being reminded of other times. Any teacher is perpetually imprisoned within his students' perceptions as a "teacher" first and a person only secondarily, if at all. This is, of course, any "student's" prerogative, if only in self-defense, just as it is the teacher's prerogative to treat a person in his class as a "student" first. The teacher's need for self-defense is greater, just in terms of numbers. He may be dealing with anywhere from thirty to three hundred students every year, while the student rarely deals with more than six to eight teachers. Perhaps this is enough to explain some of the rigidity which seems to creep into even the rare, relaxed student-teacher relationships, and which almost completely defines the tension of most of them, but it cannot explain much. Where does the rigidity come from? How can a teacher keep track of the differences between what he is and is trying to do, and his students' perception of him and his attempts? Is it possible to avoid the tension and rigidity, the cause of which is blindness and the result of which is more blindness? Is there any way to help people *see their blindness*—the blindness caused by the substitution of a social category, a name, an idea, for the person, and then wallowing in the power and the politics, which by multiple acts of this kind of substitution, come to permeate and (essentially) destroy almost every relationship between people in schools? Can't we avoid this frustration—which has locked us into a legacy of unhappiness, suspicion, and automatic antagonism? Is there any way to help students get unhooked on the system, to ease them out of their punishment-reward habit by which our schools have versed them so well in the forms and practices of addiction that at times it seems that to kick the habit would simply destroy them? Are they so addicted to themselves that for them to entertain the possibility of generosity is a threat to their being? I realize more clearly now that it had been questions like these, and my yearning to act around them, that had motivated me to help start a course, which I have now helped to teach for three years, called "Contemporary Communication" (CC to the initiates).

Teaching this course has been an experience of great variety, of great range of subject, of wide degree of student involvement—from independent enthusiasm to mass apathy, from individual stupor to group involvement. I could not tell you whether it has been a success or not. I doubt that even a very clever psychologist could devise a measure of its success that would have any relevant meaning. In fact, if I could, I would like to yell at the top of my lungs into everybody's ear that no teacher can know what he has really or significantly accomplished—momentarily, hourly, daily, yearly, or by the lifetime. Any working teacher has the duty to foster and promote a vigorous suspicion of those educationists who think they do know what they have done: if they do know, it hasn't been much (and has probably been expensive). But one cannot help being curious, and so more just to ask than to appease my feelings of uncertainty, I recently had mailed a letter to all the prior students in the course and asked them—because of this book—what they thought the greatest threats to their survival were, how they coped with them, did they remember anything helpful from CC, or anything particularly stupid we had done.

"I remember clearly one afternoon in the studio," says one student in his reply, "your asking me why I didn't 'contribute' more in class. I inferred two meanings from the question: the first was that I was not doing what I was 'supposed' to, just as I wasn't when I cut chapel or was impolite to my housemaster. That you could mean to say this angered me, as did the other insults that similarly paid no attention to individuals, but only to actors when they missed their cues. The other meaning was that it was a loss to you and the class that I didn't participate, and that you hoped I would do everyone a favor by starting. This I accepted as a real possibility, was flattered by it, but finally rejected it as a possible solution. Never did I consider the possibility that what you meant was that participating spontaneously would make me happy, and would at the same time benefit everyone else in all sorts of ways. The interpretation I chose was the safest: by concluding that your question was a reproof—that is, another thinly masked insult—I felt justified in maintaining my cynicism—maintaining a safe distance that guarded against any further mistakes I might make by saying something out loud."

You see how it is. With teachers and students things often get turned upside down—just because they happen in school. Upside down, inside out, and round about. Although my memory of this event is clouded, I do remember it happened outside of class, some afternoon when he dropped by the studio and I was feeling relaxed and said, out of some motive of vague good will and an awareness that here was a bright student I liked who didn't say much in class, that he should maybe say something in class—and he records what happened: by a logic of emotion that is neither abnormal nor unintelligent, what I thought was encouragement became, to him, an insult. Multiply this kind of incident by the number of students you teach, and that number by the number of days in a school year, and you can begin to see why teaching is both mystifying and tiring, as is being a student. And why a cross-perceived misunderstanding such as Ethan and I had just experienced didn't particularly upset me, or as I reflected on it, even surprise me.

Such reflective calm has to be earned, though, and is all the harder to have as one's relationship is closer. For example, confusion and embarrassment are my more usual companions whenever I go to discuss one or another of my own sons with one or another of his teachers. Confusion comes from the fact that I am also a teacher and know that in the ordinary language of parent-teacher conferences, urgently shaped by parental curiosity on one hand and pedagogic ambition on the other—each a complicated mixture of emotions and sensibilities, each a tangle of blindness and insight —the important things can barely be deciphered, much less mentioned. Embarrassment comes from my recognition that both parent and teacher must pretend otherwise, pretend that we know what is happening with the boy, and that all is well between us. If I don't go along with the pretense, I risk injecting further complexity into my son's life, starting the very next morning. My son is daily kidnapped, after all, and the ransom I must pay is clear: assume the best. The teacher is only the messenger at this time, come to collect the payment: he or she, too, is held under threat and has even less prospect of escape than my son.

So we talk, occasionally struggling toward some truth, each knowing, feeling, how far away from the child we are, how centered in our adult world, how little what either of us has to say relates to the triumphs and vicissitudes of our lives or his: essentially we are running on hope and whatever confidence we have in the endurance and efficacy of our own good will. The child's life is his own, and neither of us has much idea what it is—so divided and disparate is our experience of it, so filtered by our own selves, so ludicrously inadequate our language to begin even to guess about it.

A conspiracy of hope. The teacher and I are in sublimal warfare against our mutual bondage, the unavoidable, thoroughly penetrating system of assumptions which puts us just where we are, gossiping about a mutual acquaintance, our child, pretending (as all gossips must) that we know what we are talking about, that our intentions are the best. In succumbing to the temptation to be pleased together when our mutual acquaintance "does well" in the various categories which have been laid out for us to discuss, we are doing our job, performing our expected duty. Yet within us we share the recognition that, really, the less said the better. We both know that all this palaver moves us further away from our best capacities to love the child, and in so doing will later—tomorrow or the next day—move the child himself further away from his own capacities to love. There is no savor in our discussions of grades, of test scores, of "behavior problems," of "leadership capacity," and they tend to be brief. So far, our conspiracy is successful.

We are not yet at ease, you understand; we have declared a moratorium, a state of mutual disarmament in which we forego the more overt weapons which have been developed systematically to destroy our perceptions. Yet we are still confronted. I still want to know about my son, and in a deep sense to be reassured that my familial hopes have in some way been fulfilled. The teacher wants to know that her efforts—laborious, exhausting—have not been in vain. Our hope now conspires against us. Neither of us alone can know about the child, but perhaps together we can create a knowledge, a completeness that will satisfy both. Our discussion changes. We speak more about the child's social relationships, his behavior at home, our sense of his happiness and sources of worry, groping for ways in which each of us can help the child for the other's sake. How can we at home reinforce what the teacher wants? How can she be more sensitive to the sides of our child's personality that we are more sensitive to and so, in a way, extend our perceptions a bit beyond the family?

The discussion is again brief: our views are too disparate, and we only serve to remind each other of our ignorance of the child. Where before it was our hope that silenced us, now it is our despair: each new remark forces the other to realize the limitations of his knowledge of the child, raises the specter of having been wrong too many times in the past, and unresolvable worry about the future. How, if one is so ignorant, can one take any action toward the child at all, particularly of a coercive nature? One may be totally wrong! And yet, today, tomorrow, each of us will *have* to take such actions: they seem so unavoidably part of the condition of parenthood, of teacherhood. Given the necessity of future action, it seems best not to weaken each other's self-confidence, so we lapse into silence (or we lie, and simply force what the other says to fit our perceptions—or vice versa). In some way or other, we must leave this conference with confidence, and we so bend our efforts.

Most conferences end here, killed by something more than courtesy but less than courage: a weak mixture of hope and avoidance of despair. After all, we all—child included—must get through somehow, all we can do is our best, and if our best is not good enough? Absolutely nothing lies beyond *that* question mark, so nothing is achieved by dwelling on it. I remember one clear exception.

"Shall we tell them about the cupcakes?"

Joyce and Barbara glanced at each other, beginning to smile: they couldn't wait. Sitting at the table, littered with

coffee cups, piles of paper, ash trays, in the midst of the
colorful clutter of the teachers' room in our suburban
school, Sue and I were in the middle of a conference with
our oldest son's two fifth-grade teachers. The formalities,
slightly deadened by the emptiness of the room and after-
supper sleepiness, were over. I had glanced at a tiny piece of
paper with Ben's SAT scores on it, printed in Princeton,
New Jersey—a fact which somehow seems to mean more
than the figures. I had clumsily asked—haltingly, vaguely—
about some rumors I have heard that there was beginning to
be a "boy-girl thing" in the fifth-grade loft, and that there
were other signs of extracurricular tension. The two teachers
looked blank, and Barbara said, "Well, they are a lively
bunch, a real handful at times, but Ben seems to stay clear of
most of the trouble." And then, out of the blue, she mentioned cupcakes, and Joyce nodded, a conspiratorial look on
her face.

They had played a trick on the class. Secretly, at home,
they had cooked up eighty or ninety cupcakes and smuggled
them, the next morning, into school. At a time when the
children were grouped at tables working on some math, six
or so at each table, they had wordlessly given a cupcake to
one child at each table, rapidly distributing about fifteen
cakes without looking back, not letting the children know
that they had the slightest interest in their reaction.

"I had to leave the room," said Barbara, giggling already.
"They were so funny about it, I was cracking up and I
didn't want them to see me laughing. They just didn't know
what to do. First, they all looked around to see what the pattern was—did we give the cupcakes to the good guys? We
hadn't; we had carefully avoided, in choosing whom to give
cupcakes to, any pattern that we knew of. We gave them to
quiet kids, noisy kids, good students, our pets, our pet
peeves. And the kids knew them all, of course, so they had
no basis of appeal to justice. It was obvious some of them

were outraged, but they just couldn't put it into words. But the *funniest* thing was to see the different ways in which they coped!"

Joyce broke in. "One kid said to hell with it (to himself) and just ate the cake up: who questions fate? Another table spent five minutes very carefully dividing their cupcake up: it was a hard job because there were five kids, all arguing about equality, and besides, we had covered the cakes with a thick, gooey frosting which flowed back together. Then there was the girl who consented to share her cupcake, but only after eating the frosting off—the original ten-percenter! But the one that really made me laugh was the group that just pretended the cupcake wasn't there, didn't exist—that the whole thing wasn't really happening! They just kept on working and tried not to look at the thing. That was *funny!*"

"How'd the whole thing end?"

"Well, we let them work it out in whatever way they found, and then we had them write about it—'tell the truth about how you felt.'"

"Yes, I remember Ben saying something about it when he came home. He said he was so angry and wrote such awful things about you that he didn't pass in his paper."

"Yes, well he did pass it in, but only after I swore nothing would happen. After that, we brought out all the other cupcakes, and everybody had one, while we sat around and talked about it."

Neither Sue nor I asked what they thought the children had learned. We didn't need to. Barbara and Joyce were so lively in telling the story, so delighted with the experience, pleased with themselves, and able to laugh, that we both realized that we couldn't ask for more. It was obvious that each of the eighty children had learned something totally different, and that the two teachers knew this and not only accepted the fact but revelled in it. It was great. You see? Neither Sue nor I knew what Ben had learned, but we felt

good about the whole thing as we drove home, because
somehow, the whole situation had been real.

Real teachers begin to have real students.

Perceptual tension—the stress between differing realities
in their living, dynamic existence, as each person confronts
the world—perceptual tension lies at the heart of education,
at least when that education is real. I'm not talking about
memorizing formulae or learning how to fake yourself
and/or your teacher into believing you have "done the
work." When the stress builds up, something eventually has
to give. If it is skillfully done, the release of stress is accompanied by real growth of both student and teacher, of both
child and parent. If it is poorly done, the result will be stubborn rebellion confronting social bullying. The main thing
is to keep your cool—not for the sake of your equanimity,
but just to keep the future open. At times keeping calm requires an act of repression. You must bite your tongue and
risk an ulcer, actions for which nobody can thank you because they don't even know they happened. The rewards are
occasional glimmers, like the remarks of another student
from the same CC class as the first I quoted.

"As to what I remember of CC. I recall that the course
was the only one at Andover that didn't underestimate the
ability of students to grasp for understanding. I imagine that
everyone's reaction was different based on how much they
were willing to struggle to make the leaps that were offered.
I recall reading certain works (Agee and Merleau-Ponty)
that stretched my understanding years ahead of the rest of
the work at Andover. Perhaps the most joyful experience in
the class was the realization that came during the final weeks
of projects that my brothers, my fellow students, were as capable of being as intensely idiosyncratic and creative as any
author or artist that I had previously experienced, or myself.
That in itself led to a breakdown of my need to better oth-

ers, to excel, that finally opened up the possibility of true communications. I am thinking specifically of John Watkins' music, Andre Spear's film, and Mark Allen's fable."

Any time a student can have a joyful experience is a time for rejoicing. As this person's ex-teacher, let me point out that the source of his joy had nothing directly to do with me, something to do with his compatriots—one of whom was not even enrolled in the course—and mostly to do with himself. He had somehow grown to the point where he could accept their gifts. I knew nothing about it at the time.

Significant changes are subterranean.

Real education takes place in the dark, slowly. It's not that we must allow each other—as we are each other's students—to grow and evolve "like flowers into bloom," but that we must constantly recognize our ignorance and the hiddenness of relationships, whether they be with people younger, older, or contemporary. What happens out in the open is always incomplete, often misleading, and always sacrificial: we do not learn by these demonstrations of distinction, we learn by our reactions to them, which is to say that our learning is identical with the connections we make between them within ourselves. No such connections, no learning. These connections occur in utter freedom. Among many other implications, this statement means that the student—every student—can teach his teacher. The more he realizes this fact, which is more a responsibility than it is an opportunity, the more effective a student he will be: the more he will learn. His learning occurs in direct proportion to the teaching he does. But remember that if you are going to teach a person something, the best way is to let him teach something else to you. I address this remark to students, not to teachers. This does not mean simply that you will learn the most from a teacher who is learning the most (although that is probably true), but that you will learn the most from yourself, when you become both teacher and student. It is only as the gap between student and teacher becomes internal (and thereby both hidden and transparent) that the person labeled "student" begins to learn anything. Other conflicts are merely diversionary and destructive. The politics of public conflict, of propaganda, and of perceptual manipulation are corruptions of our total capacities. If we allow ourselves to be lessened it is only because we conspire with our adversaries, those who would entice us, with one reward or another, into the masochistic stinginess of jealousy and competition, into the emotional bonds of "responsible" worry about ourselves, or, diverted by some social concern or another, into an inability to be either thoughtful or kind. There are larger disciplines than those of self-control or self-immolation, and they may be more demanding. One is the willingness to wait and see what has already happened, and to accept the astonishing changes that have occurred in people and in their relationships when in a moment of revelation you perceive that they have happened while you were in the dark. Another I have mentioned: the shocking realization that generosity is possible.

Well, I didn't spell it all out like this on my drive back to Olema. At the most—and I am guessing a little because the vividness of my memory has been defused by these subsequent ruminations—I recognized the problem, defined it, realized it wasn't new, and was left with a fragmentary curiosity about what Ethan and Andy had made of our mutual mistaking. No worry. If it still mattered, I would find out sometime.

I forgot to say that it was a beautiful day. California spring sun gently heated the air, and next to the Seashore parking lot (actually five miles inland), overlaid the flat meadow with a luminous blanket of Marchness, nose-high, which reached at least to the base of the leaf mass atop each bay tree. Each tree hung its cow-trimmed hemline to an al-

most horizontal plane below which the trunk, with a knot of
gnarled roots, radiated a shallow, conical buttress to the
ground. Each tree—there were about thirty in the meadow
—seemed intent on standing still, lest by the shake of some
branch or the creak of some wooden sinew the meadow-spell
be broken, and I realize that the cows had not just left but
had been gone for thirty years. Such calm delight, the result
of man's most successful tampering with nature, can exist
only on a farm: it is the farmer's evening reward, whether in
California, New England, or farther east.

Along the trail, which led down through the bays, I felt
no hurry: there was no compelling destination until, sitting
awkward in the grass ahead, a pedestal with a sloped, plas-
tic-covered lecture on its lectern indicated my imminent education. The shallow box contained, on the right, a painted
plaster relief map of the Point Reyes Peninsula, with a ruled
red line running NNW to SSE down Tomales Bay, along
Route 1, to Bolinas Lagoon. To the left, the text read:

EARTHQUAKE TRAIL

THE SAN ANDREAS FAULT
SEPARATES POINT REYES
FROM THE MAINLAND

WALK THIS SHORT LOOP
TRAIL ALONG PART OF THE
1906 FAULTLINE FOR SIGNS
OF THE "EARTH CRACK."

And beneath the text, a small map of the trail, an arrow
pointing to a painted spot, and at the base of the arrow the
words,

YOU ARE HERE

Sue's parents visited us last week, and her father said that in 1910 he was in school with a boy who had been in San Francisco at the time of the great quake and who told of waking up at six in the morning, right after the largest shock, to find in his mouth a hard candy which had rolled from the top of the bureau beside his bed. Strange intimation! Perhaps that was all he cared to remember. It is said that for many years after, San Franciscans spoke only of "the Great Fire" as if, by common agreement, to exorcise the demons of the earth and to suggest, at one and the same time, that the disaster had a more trivial cause—something like Mrs. O'Leary's cow—and that another could be prevented, perhaps by the proper course in public education: as if one could prevent an earthquake simply by not playing with matches! Since that time the Point Reyes Peninsula has moved NNW approximately twelve feet. Or maybe the rest of the continent has moved SSE by the same amount. At any rate, no amount of common agreement will bring them back. There are some kinds of change which cannot be stopped, much less understood. They confound common sense. I mean, how is one to "understand" that the drive from here to San Francisco is twelve feet shorter than it was in 1906? Who, or what, is being served by such a conspiracy? Should I be sad, or angry?

The next sign stood a few feet further on, by a stream.

The objective of this book, before it began, was to say some sensible things about schools and schooling. All my talk about private communication was to be introductory to that task, but you have seen the mountain of thought that came to obstruct my path. With what accomplishment? I have just become aware, in this predawn suspense, that in reaching toward a definition of schooling my hand went right through it and found a first hold on the idea of educa-

CROSS THIS BRIDGE AND FOLLOW
THE EARTHQUAKE TRAIL
WHICH WILL LEAD YOU TO THE SAN ANDREAS
FAULT AND TO SOME CHANGES IN
THE LANDSCAPE CAUSED BY FAULT ACTIVITY.
ONE OF THESE CHANGES IS BEFORE YOU:

THAT IS THE CHANGE IN DIRECTION
OF THE FLOW OF BEAR VALLEY CREEK.

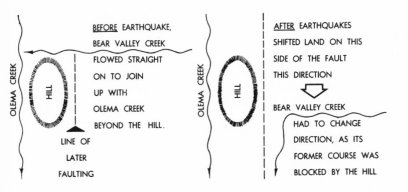

BEFORE EARTHQUAKE,
BEAR VALLEY CREEK
FLOWED STRAIGHT
ON TO JOIN
UP WITH
OLEMA CREEK
BEYOND THE HILL.

OLEMA CREEK

HILL

LINE OF
LATER
FAULTING

AFTER EARTHQUAKES
SHIFTED LAND ON THIS
SIDE OF THE FAULT
THIS DIRECTION

OLEMA CREEK

HILL

BEAR VALLEY CREEK
HAD TO CHANGE
DIRECTION, AS ITS
FORMER COURSE WAS
BLOCKED BY THE HILL.

tion. In a parallel example, it makes no sense at all to examine or think about the decorations of a building, or even its total aesthetic impact, until one has tried to understand the human purposes for which it was built. In the case of a building, this involves understanding the specific shapes of its emptiness, into which or through which its human inhabitants make their will and their way, and then trying to reconstruct in oneself the motives and motions that would have been happy and free in that space. When I speak of emptiness in this instance, it doesn't matter whether the reference is to the proportioned and radiant space between and around the columns which on all sides form the portico of a Greek temple, the processional space of the Gothic cathedral which by its simultaneous emphasis on the upward dimen-

sion and the forward dimension—toward the vaulting and
toward the "high altar"—sanctifies and makes sensual religious authority in a way that people yearned for; the "functional" cubicals of an office building, which by their stan-
dardization, imply the replaceability—and dispensability—of
any of its inhabitants; or even the "emptiness" of utter darkness contained by the highly polished, opaque exterior surfaces of the Egyptian pyramids, a darkness in fact filled with
stone, but to the real mind a void full of meaning. When I
say I "found a first solid grasp on the idea of education," I
mean something similar: that education is a human function
having to do with the totality of human will and action,
meaning and freedom. Schooling can occasionally shelter
and decorate, but *of itself* means little.

Schooling is a small part of education.

I say this for two apparently contradictory purposes. First,
it seems to me we fool ourselves when we expect schools—
classes, curriculum, tests, and various other time-killing and
social-sorting processes, an endlessly proliferating and highly
expensive bureaucratic machine—to accomplish what we
care *most* about. When I say "we" I mean absolutely all of
us, unsegregated by age, sex, race, nation, whatever. What
we care most about must remain—in itself—undefined: a
transparent emptiness, an internal freedom, untouched by
violence or social coercion, in which, into which, and from
which we can dream our generous being. This internal freedom is the first victim of the successful totalitarian society
and is much more easily taken away than it is given. It is our
greatest natural resource—as a nation *and* as individuals.
Concerning this source of life, the individual and society
must not be in conflict. Second, just *because* schooling is a
small part of education, we must pay exceptional attention
to its quality. Small experiences, considered whole, are very
complicated. Since the most influential aspects of our experience are often beyond consciousness and—if we value our

freedom—beyond social control, we must not be distracted when we are learning to approach each other and the larger totality of the world.

Consider the conditions of most schooling in these terms: a daily schedule fixed and filled, the peer-group pressure constant and sometimes merciless, much subject matter superficial and pretentious, and many teachers sooner or later numbed by the horror of it all. Can you wonder that in the face of all this quantity we find little quality? Quantity costs money, and it may be, as some taxpayers and patrons of private schools say, that schooling is too expensive. Of course, taxpayers who grumble and administrators who persuade them to spend go hand in hand: perhaps if one disappeared the other would, too.

Schooling may or may not be too expensive, but education is beyond price. Most of it is free. All of it is precious, and like rainbow gold, can never be grasped.

Education is a subcategory of our relationship with reality.

You saw what happened next: I reached through the subject of schooling to grab onto education, and education melted in my hand. True education, when it occurs between people, involves imagination, which is to say that if you stopped to examine those few best moments, for example, between a student and a teacher—when the student was overwhelmed by the beauty, forcefulness, dependability, and usefulness of even a small presentation by a teacher, and when the teacher, by the student's energy, enthusiasm, productivity, and general joy feels that he has, for once, actually done some teaching—if you stopped and asked them each to explain to the other what had happened in those moments of mutual generosity and why they thought it had been good, you would uncover such a disparity of judgment, such a difference of emphasis, and even stubborn disagreement about the facts of what had happened, that you would be forced to wonder if one or both of them were dreaming. Which is precisely what they were doing and why it went so well. True education is imaginary—not unreal, but clearly of the unhampered mind. It defies definition. Besides, it is different for each of us.

If our nonimaginary personal isolation and our imaginary connections guarantee that there are as many different human realities and as many different commitments to life as there are people, so be it. If these facts are sufficient to guarantee the mutability, the mortality, and even the madness of all social organizations, especially of those which ignore them, so be it. It is neither science fiction nor apocalyption to acknowledge the possible demise of the human race: depending on how we went about it and the pointedness of our intentions, it might take fifty years, three months, or a day, but it is *easily* accomplished. Nobody need work hard at all. On the other hand, despite certain dreams of ease, our survival will continue to take, as it always has, our most intense efforts. In our efforts together we must realize that the possible sources of our destruction are *all* social, *all* the result of mass, interpersonal agreement, and that if we do survive, it will be because of the efforts of individuals—in concert or not—and in the form of individuals. We will survive not because somebody tells us how, but because we will find a way; not because we kill off our competitors, but because we let each other live. Survival—our continued existence, divided and granular, within the divided and granular universe—is our common concern. This concern must be divided equally and freely among us. Survival is both our goal and our means to that goal, the source of our value and the receiver of our value. Survival is at once both imaginary and real, future and present, social and singular. Survival is the direction and source of all educational concern. Education is how we learn, as individuals, to survive.

Survival defines our most basic relationship with reality.

Intensely, this survival and this real relationship with reality occur at the interface between each of us and what lies around him. That is, the key ingredients of survival, which are the key ingredients of education, lie in our *perceptions of* and *actions into* the space around us about which we are still—after roughly 500,000 years—seriously guessing. Perception and action are the central concerns of education and the pivot of all schooling. Perceptual freedom precedes all others as our basic right: there is no way to *force* the prisoner to perceive his captor as benevolent, nor is there any way to *force* a young person to perceive his schooling as generously directed toward his survival. As a matter of fact (as I have suggested in a number of ways), his schooling may be stingy and crippling.

At the heart of all important questions about education lies the question of personal internal space and empty time between a person's exposure to new pieces of the world and his significant action into it: will these actions, as they become new exposures, enhance his (and our) chances of survival? Education, then, has three inextricably linked ingredients: experience to the exposed surface of self and the universe, always a source of newness and change; the free and generous operation of the imagination in its dreaming; and human will within the constancy and shelter of our personal, internal emptiness. The relationship between these three—between the contingent universe (and our experience), our imagination, and the constancies of human freedom—must remain mysterious, but it is as each of us measures their relationship that he defines his uniqueness and value to others. At times his actions appear arbitrary and crabbed, at others amazingly free and generous. So long as we accept that he is a human being trying to survive, we can learn from him. The only proof we can require of his success is his presence; his usefulness to us depends on our ability to appreciate his distance from us.

Education is profoundly political.

Schools are superficially political. Their structures of power and accountability, the details of the gossip by which great decisions are informed, the fluctuations of style and personal ambitions, the accidents of oratory, and the very sincere untruths involved in publicity—all these are surface matters only, part of our always-present social contingency. Despite their pretensions to principle, none of them is permanent. One hundred years ago, the great struggle was to remove the operation of our schools from local politics and the vagaries of "the public will." [1] That revolution slowly succeeded with the painstaking establishment of a professional bureaucracy, and an elaborate apparatus of common assumptions, acceptable public rhetoric, and even an entirely new language with which to speak about education (albeit as much to obscure the truth as to reveal it). The presumed purpose was, functionally, to keep the classroom clear of what, prior to that time, was well-recognized, publically approved, nonproductive disruption. Now, one hundred years later, this structure of defense is being attacked from all sides and within because it has perpetrated well-recognized, publically approved, nonproductive practices of schooling. Many people are, apparently, trying to reintroduce topical, relevant concern into education, and so far, many efforts have been successful. Politics has reentered the classroom from which they were so painstakingly excluded. By what right can we be so fickle and "irresponsible"?

We derive our right from our overarching and subterranean right to survive and to be the final (and first) judge of how that is best done. The days of a single, official, bureaucratically efficient, authoritative educational method are gone, and schools which cannot live with and submit to the demands of multiple, individual perception, action, and survival are doomed to wither away. Liberal and conservative,

[1] David B. Tyack, "This Period of Ferment May Be a Turning Point," *New York Times*, "Annual Education Review," January 11, 1971.

radical and reactionary, whatever their political stamp, whatever their prognosis for our future, their concern is single: survival. Not freedom, not patriotism, not rationality, not decency, not culture, not authority, not power, not dispute, not debate, not long hair, not sexual mores, not even a college education or social status. No, the issue is survival, and these others derive whatever importance they have—if any —from that issue. If we cannot agree on that, but insist on frittering away our time on superficial politics, we will not only destroy our schools, we will defeat our dearest purpose. It is this common need—and no other—which unites us ultimately, and forces us to come to terms.

Survival has to do with many-faced reality. Reality will be single only if we do not survive. Education is for survival, and at the heart of their relationship are the distinctly human variables of perception and action. Perception and action, as they vary, define our profoundest politics—the politics of survival. Superficial conflict and arbitrary confrontation, in their greedy haggling over a political power pie, simply lessen the amount of total, free power available.

If we allow one person's reality to destroy another's; if we demand that there be only one reality; if we are unable, after this amount of human history, to live with the facts of multiple, granular, human realities, we will simply destroy each other and so ourselves. The age-old waste of stinginess!

Across the bridge, there was another sign.

Another thing just happened during, or maybe just before, this early-morning waking of mine: I found I had decided that the long essay I have been ruminating for a month and a half to fit in here, where this anecdotal "advice" is, would not be written now. All the murmuring of thought that had been pointed toward a theory of personal survival in society and had found its way onto pieces of paper in sketchy notes, lists of ideas as they had come—

WHERE THE COW DISAPPEARED:
DURING THE GREAT EARTHQUAKE OF 1906,
THE GROUND BROKE BENEATH YOUR FEET.
THAT MOST RECENT RUPTURE ALONG THE
SAN ANDREAS FAULT RAN FROM RIGHT TO
LEFT AS YOU FACE THIS SIGN.
         ALTHOUGH THE EFFECTS OF THE SHOCKS
         IN THE CITIES WAS DISASTROUS, DAM-
         AGE HERE IN THE COUNTRY WAS SLIGHT.
A HUMOROUS EXAMPLE:
A RANCHER REPORTED THAT HE LOST A
COW INTO THE FAULT NEAR THIS SPOT
WHEN THE EARTH BRIEFLY PARTED,
         THEN SNAPPED SHUT –
         LEAVING ONLY THE TAIL.

         COW IS SAID
         TO HAVE BEEN
         SWALLOWED UP
         IN THE FAULT.
THERE IS NO GE-
OLOGICAL EVIDENCE
THAT THE EARTH AC-
TUALLY OPENED UP DUR-
ING THE 'QUAKE, BUT THE
STORY OF THE COW WAS POPU-
LAR ENOUGH TO BECOME LEGEND.

identified only by a word or two—will have to be satisfied with brief reference only. You may find it hard to believe, but I herewith append (Appendix III) an outline entitled, "Outline of Thoughts About Personal Survival in Society." I might, if things had been otherwise, have called it, "Notes from Underground."

The trail led up over the hill that had moved. On the crest were three signs in sequence offering information about three different kinds of trees standing there: a cluster of bays (also called Oregon Myrtle), a large tanoak, and the last an ancient live oak, its northern bark covered with lichen, its lower branches supporting a parasitic vine of poison oak. Further down the northeast corner of the hill another sign remarked on a deposit of granite cobbles which may or may not have been brought there by a stream, on the other side of the fault, which now descends to Tomales Bay, a mile to the north. A small sign further on named some shrubs near it. Then, almost at the foot of the hill, at the point where the trail turned and made its way into the branches of an oak tree which had rerooted themselves into the ground:

YOU ARE BACK ON THE
EARTHQUAKE RIFT

TAKE CARE NOT TO STEP TOO HARD, LEST YOU
SET OFF ANOTHER DISASTROUS TREMOR!
NOW YOU MAY FOLLOW THE LINE OF RUPTURE
DATING FROM 1906 – IT LEADS TO THE RIGHT,
AWAY FROM THIS OLD RANCH LANE.

AS YOU WALK ALONG THE FAULT, REMEMBER
THAT THE STORY ABOUT THE COW BEING SWAL-
LOWED-UP WAS PROBABLY EXAGGERATED.

IMAGINE, HOWEVER, THAT THE EARTH MUST
HAVE RUMBLED DREADFULLY AS THE SURFACE SPLIT.
REMEMBER THAT ALL THE LAND ACROSS THE
FAULT LINE SHOT NORTHWEST FOR 10-20
FEET IN RELATION TO THE MAINLAND SIDE,
ON WHICH YOU HAVE BEEN WALKING.

TURN RIGHT AND WALK CAREFULLY ALONG THE
LOCATION OF THE FAULT ITSELF.
ABOUT 50 STEPS TO THE NEXT STATION.

Everywhere you look there are small puzzles. For example, here the sign said "Turn right and walk carefully" etc., yet the trail went to the left as I faced the sign. Was the sign telling a lie? No, it was merely assuming some personality: some person had laid out the trail and then walked around it writing up the texts for these signs. Or perhaps he had just made notes for the texts and then, come that evening at home, had written up the final proof, which he had then taken to the man who made the signs—or maybe it was a small factory—who had followed the instructions (without ever going near the trail and so had made several arbitrary choices—the silver color, for example—without any reference to the future environment of the signs). He had called up the first man when the signs were completed, and *he* had sent a couple of men in a pickup to get them, and when they came back, he walked the trail with them and showed them where to erect the signs. But when they came to this place, he had only waved his hand and said "here" (or maybe he himself had forgotten that he had changed his mind, or was still laughing at his little joke), so that when they came to dig the hole and stick in the pedestal and replace and tamp the earth around it, they had done it all on the wrong side of the trail; and when the sign said "Turn right," you had to figure it all out and know that it meant you should turn left —because that's where the trail went, after all—and that it was not only permitted to disobey the sign, it was actually encouraged.

Many other explanations would suffice, too.

Contradictory behavior, puzzling behavior, erratic behavior usually conceals a hidden consistency within the actor, a logic which may or may not lie beyond the reach of explicit imagination or natural sympathy. In our reaching toward each other, our contradictions often reveal the depth of our care: at its gentlest, just the faith that our inconsistency won't be held against us; at its most violent, the inconsistency suggests a desire to devalue the other's opinion of us.

To understand either kind of inconsistency—and most important, to distinguish between them—requires a penetrating perception and an eye that looks inward as well, and by accepting into one's convinced experience of reality the possibility, only, of such contradictions within one's own being, thereby accepts that fundamental unity: the unity of acceptance, the gift of identity. The unity of one's own being underlies and therefore supercedes the other's unity; when that fails, what seems the other's failure is often our own, just as the other's success is our gift to him. Out of our unity each of us can regard any "explanations" with a fundamental skepticism and knowledge of the difference between the signs, symptoms, and symbols of our existence on the one hand, and the truths of our being on the other.

By the same token, rigidities of the surface, apparent consistencies, patterned behavior that pretends to be permanent or perpetual—and trots out chapter and verse to substantiate its form—all formalism should be suspected of hiding internal change, change that for one reason or another we wish to conceal. Some of us don't like to admit that time passes, that we are older than we were, that we have become desensitized to the ramifications of newness or to the boundless renewals of memory, and that we are thereby more vulnerable, more easily fooled—a possibility that may put a querulous edge to our voice, or at least persuade us that we require of the new friend or thought more credentials than we used to. Or we too much miss what once was and no longer can be. Or we cannot accept the future: these changes, in themselves, can be felt as processes of corruption, of loss, of decay, as premonitions of our mortality. When we sense them in others we are sometimes reminded of the possible meaninglessness of the entire human affair. Sometimes—in the most obvious revelation of worry about ourselves—we ridicule age, as if these people growing old around us were conspiring against us in some evil parody of hope. Age and death should be private affairs, we say, while to the world we should present an immortal face. Is the origin of this absurdity a Greek political theory that we should inhabit a city of gods or be a nation of kings? Or is it a leftover Christian hubris by which we declare that the whole notion of mortality is repugnant to us, and that we *disapprove* of death? No, time still passes and mocks mockery.

Just because we discover that, contrary to some common assumptions, both man and society are mortal (instead of just man), it does not follow that we must kill them both as soon as we can. For all its inconsistencies, individual human life may have some significance. It is possible that as each of us accumulates experience and digests it, his age may bring some kinds of gentle wisdom, resistance to violence, and consistent concern.

WHERE THE FAULT LIES

THE OAK YOU CLIMBED ACROSS MUST HAVE
FALLEN DURING THE 1906 EARTHQUAKE.
NOTE THE ROW OF OLD FENCE POSTS
THAT CROSS THE FAULT HERE

THE SUDDEN   AND MOVED THE
SHIFT ALONG   LEFT HALF
THE FAULT   AHEAD OVER 15
BROKE THIS   FEET
FENCE

SINCE THE 'QUAKE, ERO-
SION HAS REDUCED THE
FAULT LINE TO A SIDE HILL
TERRACE -- RUNNING FROM
HERE TO THE BIG RED
BARN. THE 'QUAKE SE-
VERELY DAMAGED THE
FORMER BARN, REBUILT
IN THE 1940'S, DIRECTLY
ASTRIDE THE FAULT.

Some people never learn! Imagine building a barn right where the last one tumbled, split in half by the contradictory movement of the earth beneath, its foundations betrayed by the strength of their rooted loyalty! Yet I can suspect a cagy strategy here, a momentary flash of insight from an off-planet perspective from where the opaque, thin surface of the earth over which, like so many specks of information, we humans are seen to participate in its enigmatic message and thereby know how to be baffling: maybe the farmer rebuilt the barn here not in order, by what we often call human logic, to deny the possibility of future land shift by pretending the last one hadn't happened, nor by loading this small area down with cows to prevent it, by their inertia, from moving again, but on the principle that lightning will not strike twice in the same place. He thought the chances of the fault breaking the upper surface at precisely the same place as before fewer than the chances that it would treat somebody else at least as badly next time.

They rebuilt the barn but left these fence posts here—as a reminder? Or did they just not get around to fixing the fence? Another suspicion shocked me: were these weathered posts really more than sixty-five years old, or had some of them been replaced since that time? A strange mixture of feelings confused me for a moment at the thought of such a public deception, but I resolved them—or they resolved themselves. I accepted without question that a farmer had the right to replace a rotten fence post without a second thought or any respect for its antiquity. Therefore, if this particular fence—the sole duty of which was no longer to keep the cows on one side of it but to stand and signify, dramatically, that one day the earth had moved—if some of its posts rotted at the base and fell over, they should be replaced just to remind us. Even if some of these posts had been put into the ground in 1934 or in 1959, I would not call them fake. It was their displacement that mattered. As I turned away I hoped that no man would let his demand for antique authenticity stand in the way of replacing them: their broken sentry line was an important monument.

It would be well to remember, you folks out there steaming in some political stew, that in the last eighty years there have been umpteen real revolutions: in physics, in philosophy, in psychology, in music, in architectural design, in painting, in business, in economics, in medicine, in warfare, in the application of law, in literature, in the theory and practice of engineering, in mathematics, in every known science—and the creation out of nowhere (it seems) of several new ones. These revolutions have been drastic, they have been thorough, and they have entirely overturned our perceptions of what is real. They have come, almost entirely, out of the purpose and energy of the middle. Few of them have been contributed by radicals of either persuasion, and none of them have been produced by violence, nor achieved without paying the necessary human prices. They cannot be understood by ignorance, but in our laziness we can easily forget them. Their achievement has come from a monumental effort of the middle. To let them relapse into the soup of mediocrity would be a tragedy of the middle: yet this is a much greater danger than is presented by any color of political extremism. Learn these revolutions and mark them well: they have already happened.

Back toward the parking lot, the last sign stood next to the stream, just before the trail recrossed it.

Several years ago Senator Aiken of Vermont said that the solution to our problems with the Vietnam war was simply to declare ourselves the victor—if that was what we wanted —and leave. We are now, finally, beginning to leave. It may be late, but that is always better than never. The war will end, as all wars always have, some time. Not a few politicians are banking on that certainty.

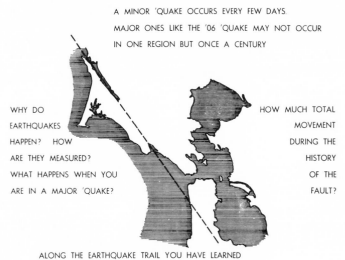

WHEN, WHY AND HOW

WHEN WILL THE NEXT EARTHQUAKE OCCUR?
WE HAVE NOT LEARNED HOW TO MAKE
THAT PREDICTION

A MINOR 'QUAKE OCCURS EVERY FEW DAYS.
MAJOR ONES LIKE THE '06 'QUAKE MAY NOT OCCUR
IN ONE REGION BUT ONCE A CENTURY

WHY DO
EARTHQUAKES
HAPPEN?   HOW
ARE THEY MEASURED?
WHAT HAPPENS WHEN YOU
ARE IN A MAJOR 'QUAKE?

HOW MUCH TOTAL
MOVEMENT
DURING THE
HISTORY
OF THE
FAULT?

ALONG THE EARTHQUAKE TRAIL YOU HAVE LEARNED
SOMETHING ABOUT THE SURFACE FEATURES
RELATED TO THE SAN ANDREAS FAULT.
RESIDENTS OF CALIFORNIA ARE PARTICULARLY INTERESTED IN
KNOWING MORE ABOUT FAULTS AND THE HAZARDS OF EARTHQUAKES.
SEVERAL ORGANIZATIONS ARE BUSY LEARNING NEW THINGS ALL THE TIME.
YOU ARE INVITED TO TALK MORE ABOUT
THE SAN ANDREAS FAULT WITH A PARK RANGER.

But the question remains real whether, with the war's end, peace will come. We are still left with a social revolution, a prickly polarization, a great deal of injustice, and a load of guilt. Peace has always had to fend for itself.[2] Maybe we should take a leaf from Senator Aiken's book, simply say

[2] "War is but a training, compared with the active service of his peace." Thoreau, *Journals* I, 247.

that the social revolution has been won—its most significant existence is mental, after all—and declare a state of generosity. The source of peace lies between each two of us: it can be lost and regained at every moment. Perhaps if we eliminated violence between each other as individuals no violence would remain in the world. Are we prepared to know the difference between violence and change? Is that knowledge what peace is?

Remember, if you really change what you really think the world really is, you really change the world—but in a different way.

I stopped, on my way back, at the Seashore headquarters. I bought a couple of geodetic survey maps of the peninsula, and checked the seismograph which stood next to the door. I wanted to see if there were any traces of the shocks we had felt the day before, but the paper on the drum, on which the sensitive needle traced its spiral course, had been changed that morning, so I couldn't tell. That evening, on the CBS local news, a report said that on the previous afternoon two Navy jets had created several sonic booms which were felt from Half-Moon Bay to Stinson Beach. So *that* had been the cause of my anxiety? Those jerks!

In the last moments of this early-morning reverie, what occurs to me to say to you is that if you want to be educated, you are going to have to educate yourself. Nobody else can do it for you. To expect somebody else to do it is like expecting somebody else to live your life.

My best advice is: don't take any advice, up to, and including, this.

6 Footprints

I TOLD you about writing to our students in the course called Contemporary Communications. Mainly I asked the following questions:

"Specifically, how do you remember the course? In and out of class, how did it relate to the rest of your life at the time? What did you enjoy, what did you dislike? What made sense at the time, what has made sense since, what has never made any sense yet?

"In addition, do you have any suggestions for a survival manual? In your experience, what threats to your integrity and growth have been the most serious, and how have you combatted them?"

I sent out twenty-nine letters. One returned "address unknown." Eleven students responded. Their replies follow. I answered each reply. Where more than one reply is listed for a student (in the case of number two, for example), this means that he answered my second letter. In every case I was the last to correspond.

Historians, or at least history teachers, speak of "postholing," a method of tackling the study of history (particularly with novices) by delineating a short period of the past and digging into it within those confines of time, uncovering layer by layer the intricacies of historical connection, hoping by penetrating deeply below the surface to indicate and thereby recreate the complexities and richness of the educated historical consciousness. Then they jump over a ways, perhaps a century, and dig again, hoping to reinforce the student's sense of richness and to suggest (but not enter) the soil between postholes by stringing the wires of a few generalizations overhead. The intent is to avoid the superficiality of generalizations alone, which remain meaningless and airy —as well as boring.

By the following letters I hope to move a step further away from generalization. I refuse, beneath their marks, to uncover anything. I will not try to dig, because, as you know by now, to say I could would be to suggest an understanding I do not have. I would, in truth, be lying. It is not just that the past that is represented here is too recent for relaxed perception. It is more that I do not mean to suggest the past at all, but at least the present—if not the future. So, instead of postholing, I offer a new procedure.

I call it "footprinting."

What you have here are some recently made marks on the sand, each of which suggests that, for a moment, a man put his weight down here and moved on. I hope that you can find some pleasure in that fact alone. Certainly, on islands of solitude, the slightest signs of human life seem enormously important.

1

Dear BBob

Your letter has done more to aggravate me than anything else in quite a while, but now that the initial waves of hostility have passed, it will be good for both of us if I recollect a few things. Quick before the next tide.

I remember clearly one afternoon in the studio your asking me why I didn't "contribute" more in class. I inferred two meanings from the question: the first was that I was not doing as I was "supposed" to, just as I wasn't when I cut chapel or was impolite to my housemaster. That you could mean to say this angered me, as did the other insults that similarly paid no attention to individuals, but only to actors when they missed their cues. The other meaning was that it was a loss to you and the class that I didn't participate, and that you hoped I would do everyone a favor by starting. This I accepted as a real possibility, was flattered by it, but finally rejected it as a possible solution. Never did I consider the possibility that what you meant was that contributing spontaneously would make me happy, and would at the same time benefit everyone else in all sorts of ways. The interpretation I chose was the safest: by concluding that your question was a reproof—that is, another thinly veiled insult—I felt justified in maintaining my cynicism—maintaining a safe distance that guarded against any further mistakes I might make by saying something out loud.

There was little I didn't regret having said in CC, save the things that went unheard in the din. Because reactions were almost never positive or constructive—my own certainly included, yes—and when someone did agree, the point agreed upon was generally lost as it became only the point of departure for another person's totally unrelated comment. As for disagreement, which can also be very constructive, it generally took the form of intellectual snobbery, or just derisive scoffing.

And you, Bob, laughing when we were floundering—which we (I, if no one else) always were—yet never helping out. When did you try to tell us how we were keeping each other down, or tell us somehow that you *really were* on our side, or point out somehow in what ways we were afraid of each other?

Now comes this letter, when you want some evidence so you can write up the experiment. And still nothing to "offer." I think to inspire trust with people there you must lay something on the line: yourself, by being open and honest—something you encourage but did not practice very much.

These are some thoughts. They are few enough to be able to fit into a breath. You are free to publish them, edit them,[1] show them to your friends. They're yours for keeps.If you have any questions, comments, requests, I will try to accommodate—between tides, of course. By no means do I feel I've finished—but it's late, you know.

Meanwhile, I left school very shortly after I came in 1968, and returned this fall. Most of the two years away I spent in S. E. Asia. I look forward to having a chance to tell you about it sometime.

Yours,

2   was, first, a large envelope containing a thick manuscript (which I do not include here regretfully); a small, dirty notebook full of addresses, telephone numbers, notes (graffiti seen on his journey); my letter and the enve-

---

[1] I have edited all these letters. In doing so, I have restricted my excisions to repetitions within each letter and to material which referred to matters of less general interest. R.A.L.

lope in which I sent it; and the following letter, together with its mirror image printed on the back, the piece of carbon paper beneath it turned the wrong way, and a blank piece of paper beneath that, originally intended as the carbon copy but forever frustrated now:

February 1, 1971

Bob:

Congratulations! You are the lucky winner in the CC sweepstakes, sponsored by the US Postal Service under supervision of President Nixon. Another, or am I the one and only, ex-cadre has been located.

CC, as the enclosed should indicate, sticks with us all. Too bad pig places like Andover are hip.

Please be careful with the journal: read it and return it registered mail. It is my only copy of my experience and more precious than even bubbles to me. I would appreciate any critical notes or thoughts you might want to append to it in its present form. I still remember how voluminous ie long-winded and perceptive ie absurd your CC comments always were.

Incidentally the most important thing I learned in CC was how to bullshit. A very dangerous thing to teach people. It goes like this: what I'm saying is true, but he thinks it's bullshit. Therefore I will stop telling the truth and start to bullshit. Since he now believes I am no longer bullshitting, I will start telling him the truth. Ad horrendum.

O'Rourke's (real world all night diner in Middletown Main St.) is hip to knowing how to tell the truth.

March 17, 1971

Dear Mr. Lloyd,

I have just reread your responses to my writing and realized how appreciative I really am of them. They have helped in many ways. I am glad that you took the trouble to respond at such length; I feel perhaps released from much of the awkwardness that I found in my attempts to communicate to people like you when I was at Andover. Perhaps it was ignorance, maybe distrust and some fear of other people that I still remember as the worst part of Andover.

As I mentioned before, I have been trying to collate my experience of last year into some sort of readable whole. For others to read, yes, but I doubt for publication. My feelings about this writing have gone from something of an Ageean passion all the way to a complete rejection of all my past experience. But I was thinking about it again today and felt a real though somewhat detached enthusiasm for writing about it. But who knows where the time will come from?

Wesleyan has been getting me down recently. But I have very definite plans to spend next year working in Vietnam, and for immediate purposes, there is spring vacation beginning on Friday.

Good luck and best wishes.

3

February 9, 1971

Dear Mr. Lloyd,

I have just finished rederiving the solution to an equation quadratic in two variables, using two well-known properties of Fibonacci numbers. In clearing my desk I came across your letter of last month. I decided to wait until classes resumed and things were operating smoothly before attempting to reply. Grades for the first semester were pretty good. In math, biology, and chemistry, which I elected to take on the "ABC/No Credit" grading system, I scored A, B, and C respectively. My fourth course was one of a different variety. There is at Brown a series of seventy-five courses open in limited enrollment to freshmen and sophomores. These Modes of Thought courses cover all subjects from pure mathematics to models of society and are conducted in much the same manner as our CC classes were—that is, informally with emphasis on group participation.

I recall deciding on CC for my English 4S course after the provision was made for a wide choice of studio courses. By the end of the trimester, I was somewhat disillusioned at the format of the course. The relaxed atmosphere was superb, with coffee, exotic tea, tennis-racquet chairs, and a myriad of cats. But little else seemed different. A book was assigned, a class devoted to those parts which were read (or not read), and a short paper of sorts dealing with the author's style would be expected shortly thereafter.

Then came the winter term. The new computer facilities had come with it. This great event, coupled with an incredible burst of energy from the CC-9 seemed to outdo the normally disastrous trimester, an American history failure notwithstanding. The idea to put Andover in a box[2] was a different one and generally speaking was attacked with great enthusiasm. Steady progress was made and reported throughout the first several weeks of the term, but toward the end, Mort came to the realization that he had three or four other courses to handle and that painstaking printing, typing, lettering, and editing the finale would have to take back seat to Teddy Roosevelt's foreign policy and the laws of thermodynamics. Most of us had put a lot of imagination and time into the preparation of new expressions of common media. Games, sound tracks, photographs, and poetry were not invented by CC, but were given entirely new perspectives with respect to our school.

It is difficult for me to tell just what the course did for

---

[2] He refers to an attempt to express their experience of life as students in a number of media—pieces of writing, photographs, sound tapes, games—which could be assembled within the volume of a shoebox. R.A.L.

me. The studio part in animation allowed me to pursue an interest in photography as well as to spark my imagination. To be honest, aside from the unusual winter, what I got out of the course is proportional to what I put in—not a lot. I must admit that most of the reading that I did do—Kafka, Heller, Vonnegut, Brautigan—was enjoyable, though I undoubtedly missed something by not perceiving allegory. As far as I am concerned, if an author has something to say, then let him say it, but say it in English.

I will be happy to answer any specific questions not covered here if you take the time to ask them. You are welcome to use or not use any and all parts of this as you see fit. Best of luck, Mr. Lloyd.

Respectfully,

4

Dear Mr. Lloyd,

Humble apologies for the duration of time passed between the receipt of your letter and the return of even an acknowledgment on my part. There are enough facets of what I would like to tell you about education or about CC or about where I am now,[3] etc., to warrant my coming up from this hell hole to visit you in your beautiful hideout. However, at present I am somewhat immersed in the waters of—yes, well even so, I hope that I can say something of merit.

I imagine that you know something about the relative levels of consciousness in any classroom: individual, teacher, mean, and, of course, the gestalt or collective consciousness (no allusion intended). In a typical contemporary classroom, there will either be no gestalt consciousness, or there will be

---

[3] Not the hip aphorism, but geographic and educational.

a level equal to or less than the mean of individual consciousness. In CC, I found that there was consistently
(though not always) a level of collective consciousness which
rose above even the highest individual level in the class.
This meant that we were constantly striving *as a group* to
reach even a tentatively secure hand hold, and this kind of
strain, which is so exciting for an individual's consciousness
or intellect, becomes doubly (?) so when it is magnified by
bouncing around a room echoed and amplified by thirteen
other individual consciousnesses all in reasonable harmony.

What we need to establish in education is not so much a
system with which we can be secure in the knowledge that it
will teach us and not become an anachronism because surely
that system has already then encapsulated itself to death; and
certainly not a system which reaches out bloated arms to encompass (as does mediocrity) all that is newly discovered in
educational possibilities in order to present them as one pre-
sents carrots to a baby—cooked, mushed, and otherwise pre-
digested; but a non-system (such as CC was) where the One-
and-Only Juggler ("I'm the one and only Juggler and I must
be the best/I love to see the ball spin never at rest/Up
in the air and back to me/And what it will do I just can't
see . . ." from the "Incredible String Band") is discovered
by one and all to be none other than oneself (also see *The
Magus*).

Granted education has always been an acculturation process, at the same time awareness of culture can easily become
stagnation or philosophical sloganeering or just plain intellectual instinctivism (or rather nut-gathering in the abyss)
(not to be confused with *instinctual intellect*) such as is
clearly the case with Marx's theory of history and Freud's
and Skinner's theories of the mind/man figure. Mythologi-
cally the stereotypes are useful, but to impose them on
projections, physical or psychical, and of course instructional
or exploratory, and worst of all, to impose the stereotypes on

the form or structure of our learning experiences, is like sticking a baby in a box for his whole life with books about mountains so he can understand mountains.

Education as acculturation can no longer survive because the cultural rate of change has increased beyond the level of the educational system's ability to acculturate. Unfortunately, what I just said is an ad man's toy phrase and not true. Superficially, of course, it is true, but historically and psychically, our culture has never been more statically paranoid and obesely mediocre. Thus it becomes necessary to transcend both the notions of education-as-acculturation and education-as-revolution, because both leave one with a sense of having been had, and both leave one's mind in a hopelessly nondirectional beta void (beta, as in beta waves, one of the electromagnetic functions of the brain, vaguely reminiscent of static on the radio).

The notion of education as survival or for survival also seems a bit back-handed. Again one is dealing mainly in what the Chinese call positive space only. It is in the fusing of negative and positive space that a good educational expedition (notice: not a system, not a process, not an experiment) must begin. A good schooling cannot be taught by Leonardo da Vinci, Beethoven, Euripides, and the formulators of the I Ching, but these people were educated (educated themselves?) with the proper combination of physical and metaphysical anchors and psychic can openers. We continue to build our knowledge based on systems of naturally occurring phenomena, and then only to a limited degree. We ignore that which is irrepresentable, nonperiodic, or supraperiodic. We ignore totally that which grows out of negative space, that which is negatively directional and nontemporal or nonspatial. I wonder where our thinking would have gone had we not been self-locomotive and had we not had the opposing thumb. If we had been dolphins, what would our philosophies plot out and our educations formulate? Certainly not boxes. Thus a suggestion for what education of the mind must allow for. But we have also to contend with that part of man which he would like to ignore, that is, his being an animal on an animal-inhabited (so far) world. Granted, with the use of television, metal, plastic, ritalin, and other external pacifiers, man the city dweller is succeeding in creating a detached, disoriented, but otherwise happy creature.

Man must relearn. He must know to his depths how he stands in relation to his tribe, his species, his environment, and himself. This is gut knowledge, but we can mask it out easily. To know these things, man must feel them in interplay continuously, and be able to deal with them just as naturally as he now can deal with all the games of which his intellect is capable. No. Not "deal with." Accept.

Forgive the pomposity which I realize exists here. I got carried away. These ideas are skeletal and stem from three or four years' worth of energy. I hope to be able to see you sometime and talk. Until then, I hope there is something useful here.

Sincerely, belatedly,

5

February 10

Mr. Lloyd,

It was a shock getting your letter. I am answering because, as you know, I like to talk, and because CC comprised a good part of my favorable experiences last year. It is hard for me to remember any of my experiences last year. My memories seem to conflict continually. I remember the course as occasionally boring and occasionally false, but for the most part fun. The ability and opportunity to have fun in my courses was far too sparse. That's why CC was both an adventure and a blessing. It related a good deal to the rest of my life and my interests. I am an avid reader, and the course offered me a chance to read things I wanted to—Kesey, Gunter Grass, Nabokov, etc.

I disliked some of the discussion tendencies, but such is my character. I greatly enjoyed the teachers, and their friendship was more than anything the reason for the course's success. I felt that you and Mr. Owen knew me better than anyone last year. Why did you know me better? I think because of the casualness and openness of the course, or yourselves, and of the students that the course prompted. I had been classified as a "jock" at Andover, yet I didn't like that classification at all. I remember writing a sentimental paper on the fact that I thought myself an athlete, not a jock. CC gave me a chance to change as I wanted to and get away from classifications. I suppose this sounds like bullshit, too. I can't seem to think about CC without it. Yet at least it is constructive bullshit, and a little bit of constructive bullshit helped a lot last year.

One memory, a tale of the incredible at Andover, deals with the final exam.[4] Having figured out the final clue, I headed for Nathan Hale. There I found my classmates, teachers, and an incredible breakfast—unparalleled in my four years at PA. I sat and ate ravenously, but then the damn warning bells for assembly rang. Knowing our duty, yet despising it, we ran to a worthless assembly, missing a most worthwhile breakfast. It killed me.

I returned to Andover recently to visit my little brother. I had two reactions: I didn't want to talk to anyone, let alone

---

[4] For several years the final examination has consisted of a treasure hunt in which each student follows a set of clues uniquely tailored to his experience of the course, arriving finally at a meal prepared by the teachers and their wives. R.A.L.

be seen. I was ashamed to be back, lest anyone think I came
back to visit the old school. Second, I was surprised to feel
myself having no other reaction to PA. I had spent four
years there, yet everything seemed far away, foreign. I just
didn't want to be there.

How to survive? I attribute my survival to my nature. I
call it my happy-go-lucky nature. This sounds self-patroniz-
ing, but I never took anything at PA too seriously except my
desire to be elsewhere last year. I got lucky, I think, getting
into college, and my memories of Andover merely emphasize
the fact that it's over, and I'm glad, but I'm glad I went
there. I really got little out of it except for a mental state
and maturity, but in that respect I am grateful. One "had to
get through it." Is it worth it? I think so. I never had a good
year at Andover. I was changing so much, so rapidly, from
ninth to twelfth grades that something always was the matter. But I smiled, made friends, did what I had to, and got
through. Big Deal. For me, at least, it is.

I don't really know what I have said or what I have forgotten. I hope this will be of help. Andover was a threat to my
integrity. I combatted it by giving false impressions and
doing as little as possible to get by. By nature I compro-
mised my identity: Andover demanded it. But it is over, and
although my views on education are pessimistic, I feel it
rather obvious that compromising integrity is necessary.

My life is great now. I'm in love. I played soccer. I'm ma-
joring in architecture. I've got a good summer job, and the
little work I do is worthwhile. Goodbye, Mr. Lloyd—I'd
better stop some place. I think Andover needed a lot more
wine and marijuana, but so does the world.

6

27 February 71

Mister Mentor:

Once again you offer an opportunity for communication. Well, that's quite an offer if you remember I'm prone to run off at the mouth as I'm about to remind you.

I have a difficult time remembering PA much less CC and an old consciousness, the shit is fading, including the ½ cut you gave me the last month which put me on restrictions, and good memories lend an aura of unreality to four long years. Senior year is coated in a haze of acid. CC fit that year well. We were young and golden. CC gave us a chance to assert ourselves. The course was full of intellectual trivia not covered in formal courses. Unrecognized classics, obscure philosophy, contemporary trends in literature and the fine arts. As the year progressed I became disengaged from the study of these topics and more engrossed in how I related to these topics. I began more to live in CC than study. I look back at myself in that course and realize how much I was struggling to acquire an identity. Talk about confused youth, wasn't I a classic case? I still am don't worry.

I think CC was a course suited to precocious seniors. We had the opportunity to expose all those talents that PA had been "stifling." We also had the chance to show that Andover had not stifled us because our "talents" were illusory. In many respects I ripped off CC and CC ripped me off. Explanation: it was easy to cop out, to hide behind ambiguities those thoughts that I could not more adequately express, those experiences that I could not more adequately explain. This was allowed. You couldn't miss a point of argument in a thirty-point essay when the final was your thoughts, period. Think, communicate, go on a treasure hunt. I was ripped off. I don't think I was ready for CC and would like to try it again. Instead I'm taking English 366: Shakespeare, English

405: Linguistics, Classics 302: Roman Love Poetry in translation, Classics 535: Greek Drama in trans., Classics 521, Mythology, History 206: Development of Wes. Civ., History 416: English History, History 526: 18th Century Europe, Honor Seminar in Far-Out Psych, and independent study in life. Such is education and I'm learning a lot and I'm graduating a year early to get it over with. Now I have a sense of who I am and what I want much more than at the time of CC. The best summary I have for CC is from Donne's "Satire III":

> On a huge hill, cragged and steep,
> Truth stands, and he that will
> Reach her, about must, and about must go,
> And that th'hill's suddenness resists, win so.

God, did we go about.

Well, survival and did I? The crux for me was independence and integrity of my selfhood which I am just now establishing. Parents are my big problem. My suggestion to any ninth grader who hadn't yet realized it would be the necessity to tell anyone, parent, teacher, housemaster to fuckoff if they try to keep you from what you have decided is of value. My values are finally solidifying and no one will destroy them for me. But compromise is necessary,[5] so I would tell baby brother to make sure he found value in whatever he did, but to accept the good with the bad for the irrelevant can be just as enlightening as the relevant. Trust in the future but to best prepare for it you must decide who you are and what direction you mean to pursue. Enough of the triteness. Regardless of what it means, I do exist. I study English Lit. to become a knowledgeable person. I desire to read, cook, earn money, travel and love. Others have often

[5] ". . . where herbs are plucked up the weeds many time remain"—Bale's *King John*.

seemed to thwart those desires. But now I am ready to come out of hiding and openly declare independence from others. I have played along and told myself that attempts to make me emotionally and intellectually depend on abstractions (parents, love, authority, etc.) wouldn't work. I have accepted myself. I love Marc, he loves me and we have strength in our love. The judgments of our peers no longer intimidate us as they had before. Teenagers can be very bitchy people. I know I was. Now I have acquired more toleration. Survival was two parts cigarettes, 1 part drugs, and a lot of good people. I wouldn't recommend it to everyone. Yet none knows well to shun the heaven that leads men to this hell—Shakespeare's Sonnet 129.

> Need I sign this?
> Well, now that I have run
> off I hope you can find
> something of value in
> jumbled thoughts.

7 is a xeroxed essay, with handwritten salutation, "Mr. Lloyd—see last page," at the top of page one:

My early exposure to the radically different, affluent environments at prep school and Harvard opened up many avenues of development that many otherwise regarded closed in the course of my growth in the more "deprived" tenement districts of New York's Lower East Side. But rather than teaching me how to gain more, or have much, or even to use much, this opportunity to live under such sharply contrasting economic, social, and cultural standards has shown me that the most important thing, really, is to *be* much. As far back as I can remember there has always seemed to me a great gap between the quest for attaining goals of intellectual competence, professionalism, and expertise that our technologically oriented society forces us into and my personal desire to lead a rich, full, happy life. So when I, among others, swelled the numbers and ranks at such a prestigious and venerable institution as Harvard in hopes of enriching myself with the wisdom and sensibility of its glorious past, only to discover that what modern society really wants from its schools is technicians not philosophers, the gap widened, soon to become an unworkable contradiction. Most of my actual schoolwork, by its pedantic nature, was insignificant, frustrating, and unnecessarily oppressive to me. Rigidly compartmentalized, overanalytical, striving to be "objective," it provided very little room for originality and imagination, prohibited sensitive exploration and self-examination, and was presented in too pretentious and inflexible a manner. I was too often urged to push opinion aside in the name of scholarly research, or, even more, it was assumed that I'd have to wait until I could enroll in higher or graduate level courses before I'd be able to discuss or develop my strongest feelings and thought!

Too long had my performance been judged on how well I played up to or accepted what other people thought best for me. What about my own self—if I be what others expect me to be, what do I be? A product of an educational system, serving technological demands, that is overwhelmingly literary and mathematical, which prepares every one to be clerks and bureaucrats and provides apprenticeship in arts only reluctantly, for those considered (erroneously) too stupid for intellectual advancement. If I be what others expect me to be, increasingly cut off from the fundamental arts of living and the mainsprings of my humanity, do I be what I want to be and need to be? Of course not! Federal agencies, private foundations, well-meaning benefactors, and established institutions may pour millions of dollars into solving the "problems of the ghetto" or improving the "culturally deprived," which to them means producing such bright stars as myself was becoming, but in the end, I wanted nothing more than to recapture all I'd lost in the process.

I decided to break away from what was, to a moneyless student, an almost guaranteed easy road to "success"—I left school, thereby leaving myself vulnerable to the draft (my number is 97) and all its consequences. I now feel strengthened that I made that first step—and the first step is an everlasting step—toward confronting the Selective Service System and rooting out that distress from which many young men like myself suffer. But more important is the renewed sense of confidence and enthusiasm that stepping outside habitual and conditioned patterns of development (i.e. schooling) has brought about. For by not participating in an artificial, competitive system in which my success was always the result of failure of others or of knowing and doing exactly what was expected of me, I finally exposed my true self and encountered my natural limitation. And what boundless and soothing joy this did bring! What understanding and vitality! I felt reborn—alive again, no longer dead. I also felt an inexplicable, new-found faith, later realizing that faith is, above all, open-ness, looking at life without a background of prejudice, knowledge, or experience—an act of trust in what is unknown.

It is this faith I embraced as I set out to overthrow the programming of my past and enquire into the unknown, into myself. My travels led me first to Alaska, which was disappointing at first. The experience of seeking my fortune as a firefighter only to have it rain, and then groveling for other jobs I probably wouldn't have enjoyed only to end up living on Food Stamps, still has me thinking how necessary it is to try to start creating and experimenting with alternatives to the life-styles I've been accustomed to rather than merely knocking, evading, outsmarting, resisting, or destroying the system. My emphasis, more simply, became constructive rather than destructive, more outgoing and positive rather than fearful and resistant.

More practically, I began to sort out all the illusions I had about what I wanted to do, stemming from the various "patterns of prestige" and figures of respect I'd been influenced by, the ambitions, dreams, goals, purposes, and fantasies I'd learned and created. When I got serious about it, nothing interested me passionately outside living in the wilderness, physical education and movement, the material arts and crafts, and living, working, and playing with children. I thought I might combine these someday, but I realized my more immediate problem was learning and relearning certain skills.

And on the bottom of this last page, again handwritten:

Mr. Lloyd—
Received your letter, forwarded from New York. I'm leaving for the East Coast, probably tomorrow, and as a result I'm too busy to say much of anything now. I'll try to respond more fully later on. This is a copy of my personal essay to Goddard College, to which I'm applying as a transfer student. It's the most I can offer now.
                    Cheerfully yours,

8 is an air letter from India:

In re CC circular:
It's raining just enough to bring out the rich smell of earth and grass, of pine needles and wood, to give the early evening air a fresher coolness halfway up to the roof of the world (If I were a king of Tartary/ Me and myself alone/

My bed would be of ivory/ Of beaten gold my throne) on the highest mountain road terra has to offer, surrounded by evergreens and snow-capped spikes, waterfalls and fairytale cobblestone paths through wild grass and flowers past bursting streams and grazing long-haired mountain goats.

I'm in Manali-Himachal Pradesh, a stone's throw from China (or Chinese-administered Kashmir). Just finished a year studying Sanskrit and Telugu at Andhra University, Waltar, A.P. Also completed a magnum opus, "Symptoms of Psychosis in an Indian Mental Hospital," first research of the sort on the subcontinent. It involved three months of interviewing patients in a rural State Hospital.

Now about survival: some people respond to electro-shock. Personally, I try to avoid artificial stimulation.

I'd enjoy talking with you about CC and survival if you're still interested.

Hope all is well with you.

9 is exceptional in that his first letter preceded mine.

December 26, 1970

Dear Mr. Lloyd,

I heard from Mr. Owen that you were residing in state. It is a curious coincidence that we should be in the same area at the same time. It was last year, after my first freshman semester at Brown, that I took a leave of absence with the intention of justifying myself to myself in an environment conducive to uncluttered peace. Resigning from the society of friends here at home, I began to read some books that were long overdue in my life—Plato, Tillich, Gibbon, to name a few. An informal trip through California, Utah, and Nevada on boxcars, and an excellent tour through Europe helped cement a growing understanding and acceptance of my particular approach to life. I've been able to establish basic assumptions (limits) by which my freedom may be defined.

One of the most important accomplishments was a twenty-four-page essay on my beliefs which culminated in an application for conscientious-objector status. I've already been rejected once, so I am attempting to get as many references as possible in support of my application. I'm hoping that you will be able to write one for me, since you were a teacher and a witness during some of my most important philosophical developments. It is philosophical outlook that interests the draft board most; they want to know if my beliefs are and have been an important part of my life, and if I am sincere (and/or religious). Much of my thought was developing during my eleventh-grade year and solidifying during my senior year at Andover. Curiously it is only now, after having been alone, that I have developed the strength to live those thoughts. I have included some more recent (but not unrelated) conclusions with this letter. If you would like to write a letter in my support, it should include (1) who you are—your occupation, etc., (2) your relationship to and experience with the applicant (me), and (3) your feelings about the applicant's character, his sincerity, and the strength of his beliefs. I have included the long essay and a short summary of my beliefs to help you in your evaluation should you choose to write it. Also since we are in the same general vicinity I would like to drop up and see you—when convenient—to talk about this and other things.

(He included, as he says, a lengthy summary of his philosophical position. I sent along a recommendation and, later, my letter about CC. He answered:)

February 14, 1971

Dear Mr. Lloyd,

If this is indeed a treasure hunt, will I find steaks (stakes) at the end? In fact, it does sound like the great CC Treasure

Hunt. All of us poor mockeries wandering around looking for steaks . . . godamn . . . I guess we're the only living things on earth that know how it's all going to end up anyway.

Besides my irrevocable, incorrigible penchant for that course of action which best reflects irresponsibility, the reason I have been delinquent in my contemporary communications is that I've been preparing for my appearance before the draft board, which was scheduled for Feb. 10. My lawyer remarked that I had one of the most complete and disciplined files he had ever seen, that he could not think of any reason that they should refuse me, I interviewed the board for forty minutes (most personal appearances last no more than ten minutes), I had fantastic letters—including your "Charles . . . is not simply perverse" (which *did* make me laugh)—I had two adult respectable witnesses present at the board (the board refused to see them), and I answered all of their pathetic and simple questions with an aggressive humility (?) and afterward I congratulated myself on an excellent presentation. Nevertheless, this morning, I received—again—a reclassification of I-A which means that they don't believe the letters attesting to my sincerity or to the overwhelming evidence of the profundity of my beliefs. But Onward and Upward. Next stop is the state appeal board, which will refuse me. Then if I get called up, since I'm not going, it will go to court, where if the judge, if he ever read a book in his life, will get a good laugh out of it. Or maybe I expect too much.

In defense of my long essay, it was organized in such a way as to answer four questions: what are my beliefs and why are they religious? what is my religious training? why don't I want to be a medic? and in what ways have I given expression to my beliefs? I wrote it with the hope of communicating some vital ideas to the board—hence the doctrinaire tone of the thing. I do have doubts and leave myself open

for better approaches, but this is the best I have come up
with so far. Cut through the verbiage of eight months ago
and I find a consistent statement that there are various ideas
which, because they participate in the general and eternal
truth of mankind, transcend my body in importance, and
that they are the basis for all personal truth. Which means
that I acknowledge certain ethical limits beyond which my
physical existence is meaningless and undesirable. My nature
is a totality—a togetherness—with all functions functioning
simultaneously and indivisibly. The given is that I am always in control of all these functions, and the result is that
whatever I do at any given time is necessarily right.

I think I may have made too much of the body-soul division, with the stress on the faults of the body. In truth, the
two are coexistent, and complementary; the soul (field of
conceptions) is given ontological force only by the body
(field of perceptions), while the body is given direction by
the soul. My contention is that conceptual truth is greater,
and more basic, than the perceptual truth, i.e. take a great
work of literature: the number of pages and the size of the
print is far less important than the ideas put forth therein.
The conceptual is not limited to the present time-space as is
the perceptual.

As to the relationship between sensitivity and Truth: the
more sensitive, the closer to the Truth; the closer to the
Truth, the more sensitive.

Your query regarding how much despair I've experienced
is a difficult one to deal with. Sufficeth it to say that I felt J.
Alfred Prufrock was a relevant archetype, and that it was as
close to despair as I would like to come.

CC. CC was a mixture of security, novelty, personality, in-
trospection, and creativity all directed at the question who
am I. I felt secure in the sensitivity and concern of Lloyd,
Owen, in the uniqueness and elevation of the course (we had

to do some academic work so our elevation wasn't totally un-warranted), and in the rapport with other students. It was the one class in which I had a definite feeling of belonging. At the same time, the uniqueness and elevation inspired eli-tist-take-for-granted relationships which often ignored indi-vidual sensitivities.

Now and then flexible approaches like the parables, the double lecture, the collage, *Magus, Volcano,* open black-boards, *Godot, Rhinoceros,* and the final exams allowed us the privilege of breaking new ground. On the other hand, the old academic approach like *Hamlet, Rosencrantz,* Mer-leau-Ponty, and *Irrational Man* to name a few while making us more comfortable in PA terms (less guilty) tended to take us apart. With the new approach the stress was on the stu-dent, so that each personality became amplified.

CC brought me closer to the other students by watching them relate their personalities with group subject matter—a relationship which falls somewhere between academic dis-cipline imposed on the student, and his own creative space. Such a relationship can neither be found in other classrooms nor outside of class. The external manifestations had corre-spondingly greater internal reactions. There was a disparity between the sensitivity I had for myself which rendered me unable to respect the others' sensitivities. CC, devoted as it was to communication, inspired my communicative dilem-mas to become obnoxiously apparent, externally. Since each obnoxious appearance also debuted in front of a host of baseless introspective judges (within the mind), the whole course became an introduction to myself.

While these dilemmas dominated my thought, the struc-ture of CC provided various answers-directions. I didn't find any direction at the time; in fact, paralysis continued down-ward until the bottom dropped out in the fall of '69. But it did provide me with a greater awareness of my problems, and indeed, when it came time to start upwards, such CC

projects as Merleau-Ponty, *Irrational Man,* and the mini-
essay-poem-short story that I wrote became important guides.

I haven't done CC justice so I'm going to have to come up
and talk to you.

10

February 11, 1971

Dear Mr. Lloyd,

Your letter arrived on the heels of another money request
from Andover and so set off in me the usual (and perhaps
unusual) train of reminiscences. Your letter was the first intelligent attempt at a followup of the *learning* experience
that Andover was for me, and as such I will reply with as
much honesty as I can summon.

Let me initially tell you briefly what I have been doing
since I left PA to clue you into some of the context of my
thoughts. After an initial radicalization at Columbia in the
mutually violent hands of SDS and New York Tactical Police Force, I realized that what freedom of political expression ever existed in this current had better be expressed co-
vertly (underground) or the activist was opening himself up
to social brutalities that would permanently scar his ability
to deal rationally with the political structure. I pursued sociology as my discipline towards understanding and was able
to study with Daniel Bell before he left for Harvard. I have
followed up in that field with much intensive effort in an attempt to understand what forces both internal and external
make us into a society. There is much that I could say about
this but will put it off for a while. In February of 1970 I left
with Mary Thomas (she sang with you for a while) and John
Watkins for Central America. John left after two months,
and Mary and I continued into Mexico and Central America

for six months more, living with various peace corps people, Indian villages, medicine men, etc. The overt reason to go on the trip was to study the role of religion in native American social systems; the personal reason was much more one of survival. I wanted to get out of the mainstream culture of America and learn about the enculturation of the western hemisphere as it has existed for twenty thousand years. My desire was unknown to me at the time. I just felt a lack of direction and a blunting of my ambition that I could not place. The experience in Central America was almost daily deepening and clarifying my perception of the value systems and cultural arrangements that were attendant with my position in society.

We came back from Mexico in September of this year. Sometime during the trip I had decided that sociology was good for me only as an objective expression of my understanding, and that my personal desires inclined much more to service. In line with that realization and a desire to find some skill or profession that would let me continually increase my knowledge of myself and others, I made the decision to study medicine. I am currently at Columbia again studying the prerequisite sciences and applying to medical schools in the southwest. I have been working for some months in an effort to set up drug-rehabilitation programs, community health services, and para-professional medical personel in New Mexico. I look forward to the studying and practicing medicine because I feel that I will truly have a discipline within which I can both serve others and grow myself.

As to what I remember of CC. I recall that the course was the only one that I took at Andover that didn't underestimate the ability of students to grasp for understanding. I imagine that everyone's reaction was different based on how much they were willing to struggle to make the leaps that were offered. I recall reading certain works (Agee and Merleau-Ponty) that stretched my understanding years ahead of the rest of the work at Andover. Perhaps the most joyful experience in the class was the realization that came during the final weeks of projects that my brothers, my fellow students, were as capable of being as intensely idiosyncratic and creative as any author or artist that I had previously experienced, or myself. That in itself led me to a breakdown of my need to better others, or to excel that finally opened up the possibility of true communication. I am thinking specifically of John Watkins' music, Andre Spear's film, and Mark Allen's fable.

There is much that I still don't understand about the course: what were your intentions for the various experiences we underwent, why the need to grade anything once the initial assumption of honesty had been made. I tried to get at these things in the final exam. I remember writing about categories of friendship, personal and professional. That was my way then of saying why, after all this shared human experience of learning, are you Mr. Lloyd and not friend Bob, and Mr. Hughes not friend Guy. I had learned in that course that lessons come wherever the light falls, not in any particular structure or from any particular person.

About survival. CC specifically taught me to jump, to be satisfied that partial understandings are indicative of future awarenesses. It reinforced, however, the whole tradition of Andover that survival is a factor of the mind. I do not think that this is true. There is a basic human ineffectuality that is engendered by Andover's approach to these questions. I have learned since that a certain amount of physical resilience and experience are far more important to developing a sense of efficacy (which is really what survival seems to be) than almost any abstract quanta of knowledge. On the other hand, access to tools (as the Whole Earth Catalogue calls it) is very important business. The ability to recognize in the transmission of knowledge what is viable and life-making

and what isn't, is very important. There might be more formal ways of stating this need for personal efficacy and use of
tools (knowledge) that would be helpful to your book. They
are beyond me right now.

You place the emphasis of your letter on cultural survival.
I think we survive our culture by understanding it. As a people we have some need of the sense of national urgency, but
I think as individuals that it gets in the way of growth. I
think that, with an historical perspective, the cultural forces
that in the main shape our development can at least be understood, if not integrated into our future growth. That is
not to say that we should keep consumer capitalism as our
political ideology, but that the development of out minds is
something slightly separate from it. Marx remarked that capitalism was a concurrent politicization of the culture. I do
not believe this to be true. We feel at various times that our
own uncertainty, doubt, fear, success, or whatever is being
shared by the political structure, but I do not think the tie is
important. Old friends of mine from Columbia SDS who are
now in the Weathermen are coming to the same conclusions,
though from a different bias. As to what might aid growth or
survival of growing crises, I can only recommend what has
worked for me, what I spoke of before, a personal sense of efficacy, faith in myself if you will, and a never-ending, sometimes neurotic desire for increased knowledge. I would put
one comment into any manual for survival: have faith in
yourself, when you are off the path you will know it because
it will nearly kill you. Carlos Castenada's *Don Juan—A
Yaqui Way of Knowledge* says this much better than I. At
Andover most of us took our direction from our brother students or professors we admired. I think a little more direction could come from ourselves, so that we could learn to
rely on our intuition and acquired knowledge.

I don't know whether this will be any help to you. I have

tried to show what I have been up to in the years since, that being the best way of letting you know what I have gained from CC and Andover schooling. Let me know how the work goes. I am always interested in thoughts about survival and growth.

11

March 4, 1971

Dear Mr. Lloyd,

I am sorry it has taken so long to respond to your letter. It reached me right at the start of the competitive ski season and since then I have barely had time to do my homework much less anything else.

Threats to my integrity. There is very little I can say as I have experienced very few if any real threats. In terms of survival, the most important sustaining device I have found is my constant optimism and the motto, *illegitimi non carborundum*. I guess I have found that a strong confidence in my ability to overcome difficult situations is also important.

Now to CC. In order to answer all your questions about my reactions to the course I have decided to explain myself in lists and brief flashes rather than whole paragraphs.

CC EVALUATION SHEET

Scales:

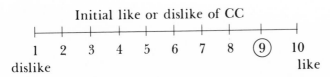

Initial like or dislike of CC

1   2   3   4   5   6   7   8   ⑨   10
dislike   like

How well did the course live up to its possibilities?

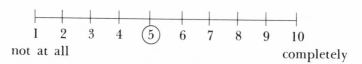

1   2   3   4   ⑤   6   7   8   9   10
not at all   completely

Explain: we did do some reading and some work, true. But we could have done much more, I think. Two reasons we didn't do as much as we should:

1. We the students were lazy.
2. You the teachers did not push us enough toward producing.

There was a lot of potential for the course which I don't think was realized. Because we were lazy I think you should have expected twice as much from us. In that way we would have produced nearer our potential.

Readings:

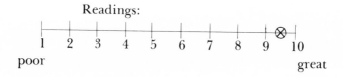

1   2   3   4   5   6   7   8   9   10
poor   great

Catch 22 still remains the best book I have ever read. And I have reread it twice. *Cat's Cradle* also was excellent. My introduction to writers I might never have read was very worthwhile and is relevant to the rest of my life. The course for me outside the reading was contemporary only to Andover, for the discussions involved mostly the Andover environment. During my senior year I found being able to talk on a more or less equal basis to faculty members (you and Mr. Owen in CC) was very important because it helped me understand Andover and myself in it from a different view point. Most student's views are remarkably similar. The course helped me to evaluate logically my experience at Andover. How was my experience? Good. Why? *Illegitimi non carborundum* and I didn't.

So much for my evaluation. I hope it has helped you evaluate CC on a broader scale. Thank you for writing.

Sincerely,

April 13, 1971

Dear Mr. Lloyd,

To clear up a few of your questions, let me begin with "illegitimi non carborundum." It means "don't let the bastards get you down." In my basic survival theory I acknowledge the fact that there are plenty of bastards all around just waiting to smash your existence. The first defense is to avoid them if possible. If not, then good humor and a slow temper will see one through.

On the question of academic pressure, I agree with you in thinking academic pressure is addictive. I also agree in the thought that as a form of motivation it is absurd. I do not "like" academic pressure. However, I have always found I have done better and learned more because of the hassles. The more one is bombarded with information the more one must learn from simple osmosis alone. So, although I do not like academic pressure, in accordance with my basic survival philosophy, I accept it for its good points and can live with it easily. The greater my work load the greater the challenge for me to push my limits and understand my capabilities. I strive toward self-actuation. The search for my own limits both physically and mentally intrigues me. I enjoy being challenged. This is why I stand on high towers and ski jump. This is why I ski seventeen miles in a cross country race. I don't enjoy it while I'm doing it, but when I'm done I can say I jumped off that tower, I ran that race and finished, I now know more about myself, my limits from that experience. In academic pressure not only do I learn about myself, but as a by-product I attain a "classical" education. Under pressure I teach myself. In order for a student to teach himself he must, in my opinion, be motivated to challenge himself. The challenge, not the grades, not outside approval or disapproval, should be the student's motivation. If one can teach a student to enjoy the challenge and then present him with a challenge, the student should be able to teach himself.

I hope this has been some help to you.

Sincerely,

7 A Parable

Boston, Massachusetts; April 15, 1970; 4:45 P.M.; at the intersection of Charles and Beacon streets:

While the last speakers with the staccato passion of an intricately partisan and ultimately boring rhetoric have attempted to nail the peace movement onto their various local causes, and then while the Boston cast of *Hair,* reluctantly allowed onto that rigidly and tensely defended platform, has tried to sing the sunshine in through a warped and tinny PA system, and then while the platform finally empties and in the late afternoon sun we more ordinary souls have straggled away to wonder what has been said to whom and young volunteers are even now collecting massed wads of waste paper in enormous plastic litter bags, and then while we wait here to meet the others who are going to drive home with us—all this while the mob has steadily and stealthily crept in small groups from the crowded Common until it fills to overflow-

ing two or three blocks of Beacon Street with hair and flashing eyes and shouts and sweat and colorful clothes which
flicker and flash over the deep mutter of its voice, a voice incapable of articulating a purpose but which, by its size and
steadiness, seems to create, or rather to speak a raw purpose
of its own—that after all that listening it will now have its
own way simply by existing in the air, in the open. And this
lank boy who drapes angled elbows and knobby knees
around the street lamp he has climbed to survey the mob
from its edge—he looks and says nothing, makes no gestures,
and so is ignored by the policemen and thinly disguised G-
men who stand or move tensely around his feet—how shall I
describe him? His profile, large-beaked and small-chinned, is
so intensified by his stylized skinniness that the crimson
stocking-cap which tops it drives his image irreversibly into
caricature, yet I cannot decide whether this is the caricature
of ridicule or the kind of caricature which reminds us that
the real is always haunted by the imaginary. Is he a Daumier
cartoon or a revolutionary poster-image? Is the steady esti-
mate of his gaze saintly or insane? He clambers down and
joins the mob as it moves off and heads for Massachusetts
Avenue and eventually Cambridge, followed in orderly array
by a phalanx of riot police—the plastic visors on round
white helmets and shouldered billy clubs strangely Greek—
and then, like so many anachronistic tumbrels, two red am-
bulances, a paddy wagon, and a fully manned fire engine.
Perhaps nobody knows it yet, but within three hours this
mob will have broken every store window in Harvard
Square, set fire to the subway kiosk, and escaped into the
surrounding streets, uncontrolled even by those within it
who protest its violence: unless some mark is made, unless
the crystallized blood of property is spilled over the street
for all clearly to see, the mob will not be satisfied. A demonstration must be made.

Boston, Massachusetts; April 15, 1970;
5:25 p.m.; on Pinckney Street, at the north side of Louisburg
Square:

Our group has assembled, and the others stand around me
in still-silent witness as I unlock the door of my microbus.
Walking rapidly up the hill, sweeping the sidewalk side to
side with his white cane, a blind man brushes by. As our
group scatters to let him pass, he holds his bare head high as
if he could see us through his dark glasses. He walks confi-
dently, almost faster than necessary—perhaps to display his
skill—barely interrupting his stride when his cane flicks a
fire hydrant, and he is by and beyond us before I realize that
I have recognized him, that fifteen years ago I lived for the
summer in Cambridge and drove out to his house on Na-
hant twice a week to read aloud to him. At that time he was
studying for a graduate degree in economics, an accommodation between his blindness and his technical interests: he
lost his sight at the age of twelve when a chemical experiment he was working on (or playing with) exploded in his
face. Since that time, he has lived in a world explored and
known only by his hands, the tip of his cane, and the words
of friends, a world limited by the reach of his arm, the range
of his hearing, and the eloquence of imagination. Through
that blackness he now strides with clear purpose. His clothes
are tidy, his body lean and exercised, his bearing relaxed,
and his face reveals no inner complaint. He is gone before I
find a voice to speak, and I realize that he has said much to
me although I have remained, for the moment, just another
of the hidden, untouched, unheard parts of his dark universe. He has been walking so, unaided even by a dog, for
twenty years or more. Against the awful threats of his environment he has not struck back, nor has he succumbed. In

the darkness of his world his value and his energy are radiant.

Should I say now that this blind man's clear purpose was created and maintained by his infirmity, while the destructiveness of that mob was the natural outcome of its clear vision?

Could I say now that the mob, just by being a mob, has proven that each man in it must be blind, while this blind man, by the extravagant daring of his lonely motion, has proven that he can truly see?

If only I could give each of them his vision, and him all their eyes!

Appendix I:

A Structural Paraphrase

ALTHOUGH the following pages could be understood as a summary—or even, for some, an explanation—of what has preceded and easily can be used either way, they are not primarily so intended. I place them here, first, as yet one more particle in the granular structure of this book. At heart, my entire effort has been an attempt to be consistent with the message of the book, to do what I say should be done.

The second reason for the following paraphrase contrasts with this first reason. Beneath the shifts and changes I also intend a consistent message, but one which cannot initially be stated in a paraphrase. The particular message I intended could only be offered in the granular form it has assumed, and for that reason the paraphrase is here, only subsequent to the text.

In addition to the fact that what follows is really two paraphrases, one more succinct than the other, it should be noted that the two are not equivalent: the shorter is not always the more abstract or distilled.

pages   III. Solo Flight

We are physically isolated,

intellectually alienated,

IV. You and Me

pages
our independence:

53–56   we must stay loose toward each other.

e.g. we agree to disagree.

56–61   For another example, in cases of strong intracultural relationships,

Before we can communicate we must measure the distance between us, even though to do so is difficult, indeed.

61–62   we must carefully measure our distances from each other, and our differences,

62–68   both as they preexist and can be seen objectively to lie between others

68–69   and as they change and are directly experienced between us.

69   Again, how can we trust that experience of the other person?

69–74   Only as we allow for the distance between us and for each other's internality—in other words, for our actuality, and the actuality of our conditions,

74–75   which are both stable (in their present and subsequent hiddenness) and thereby trustworthy, and also subject to change (in their physical and experiential variation) and thereby of renewable value.

Given enough information, any distance can be crossed.

76–82   Any distance between people can be dynamically crossed

pages

—via the expanding idea of transparency and opacity—connected to our survival (= our continued actuality).

111–115   Transparency and opacity are an endless source of freedom and constraint, but as they combine in us, they define a particular, human, mortal, speaking life.

Our situation is both idea and fact, both serious and funny, as we start, go, and stop.

115–117   To carry this idea further away from compromise and further into a world at once physical and ideal, finite and limitless,

Given our conditions, the least we can do is to learn to be generous toward each other, as well as grateful and creative.

117–124   let me point out that there are three ways of seeing communication: as radiation from the monad, as a system of feedback referring to the monad, or—best—as the creation of new granules of actuality between monads.

124–128   This last way combines elements of the first two. The message becomes in some way equal to ourselves—a new, granular part of the universe, a monad in itself, which can be given away.

128–133   The requirements for communication seen in this way are internal freedom, expansiveness, discipline, and generosity—

It is sometimes simple.

134   just as we find in nature. Don't you wonder about it?

Interpersonal relationships, social relationships, society itself—all are mental constructs and therefore subject to change: in fact, they are as hidden as our dreams.

135–136   Let me give you some advice: society is as mortal as we,

136–138   things in it change which you wouldn't expect,

139–143   especially in "authoritarian" relationships, such as happen in school.

143–147   If we treat each other as real, we will be all right,

147–150   but we cannot expect to know all about it as it happens: real learning is hidden.

We share this quality with the earth on which we walk;

150–151   Even small details of an experience can become important and attached to other larger meanings.

it is granular, too.

151   In this context,

Deep beneath our feet, the foundation of the landscape moves.

152   subterranean changes cannot be stopped: they are unreasonable and apolitical.

Whole hills and rivers move over and change course.

153   For example,

pages

**Schooling, education, even our ideas about what is
real—all these change, and we must adapt our
goals to these changes or risk our survival.**

152–155   if you start to think seriously about schools, you
must base that thinking in thoughts about education, thoughts about education must be based
in thoughts about actuality, and thoughts about
actuality must be based in actuality.

156–157   By our actuality, may I remind you, I mean our
survival as individuals, as granular beings.

158–159   Education, beneath all the rest, is concerned
with our survival. Its deepest politics is centered
on this question:

158–159   how can we survive as independent, granular
beings? What was once progressive, in the world
of education, may have become regressive in this
sense.

**Even whole cows have been swallowed alive by the
earth, some say.**

160   Some intentions, delayed, assume unexpected,
even unbelievable forms.

The story of the cow probably lies.

159–161   As I walk along here juggling ideas,

Signs get turned, disengaged from meaning;

161   look out! Things change fast.

**likewise, the meaning of human growth is hard to
keep track of, but can be good although misunder-
stood.**

162–164   See, because this particular sign is (like anything) independent, it got loose from its in-

pages

tended mooring in the human scheme—but we can still understand it. In the same way, people change in unexpected ways (and sometimes pretend that they don't); but with imagination and sympathy we can help each other through.

Apparent disasters can be recorded as simple change, and much can be maintained or restored.

164   Or another example, when we notice and report changes,

Likewise, the most serious changes occur where least expected or evident, tacitly.

165–166   we should remember that, contrary to either revolutionary or reactionary opinion, the most drastic changes in our lives have occurred at the center of society.

We wonder what changes are happening now.

167   One final example: right now

Is it possible that our society could change for the better?

166–168   we must face the fact that peace will be difficult, too, and full of new problems.

Maybe you could do it!

168   Trust yourself; listen to others.

VI. FOOTPRINTS

What do some young people say?

169–170   Let's listen to some younger voices. I will go away while you do.

pages
"Go to hell!"

171–172   1. "Teach, you're a jerk. What did you ever do for me? I've been in SE Asia, and you can shove off."

"I'm dying to figure out how to speak to you and tell you how I am floundering."

172–173   2. "Hey, daddy-o, here's my diary for the last two years. Wanna read it? How about helping me get it published? O, I remember, you're the guy who taught me how to lie."

(Lloyd response omitted.)

173–174   "Well, perhaps I was too flip. Thanks again. Here are some serious projects I'm working on now, although they (like me) are largely unappreciated."

"Here's what I think; now, back to work."

174–176   3. "I am doing as well as my grades. After all, I do like numbers. You taught me little, and I didn't work hard. I enjoyed the reading, but didn't understand it. So long."

"I can hardly keep up with my thoughts, but I'm working on them. Here are some of them."

176–179   4. "I had a great, rather mystical time in your course, which helped free me from most preconceptions about education—which I now regard as noninstitutional. I have been thinking like crazy about my education."

"I have found that if I don't get involved, things take care of themselves."

pages

179–181   5. "I don't know why I'm writing to you. That school year has disappeared into another hidden compartment in my life, to be forgotten and not renewed. In college I am now very content—physically and sexually—and have chosen a career. See ya round."

"My motto is: everybody can go to hell, especially parents."

182–184   6. "I'm a homosexual, but I'm all right, Jack. I'm working hard, plan to be comfortable and to lead a pleasant life. I have had a life's worth of suffering already."

"I have wandered a lot, and am still wandering."

184–187   7. I'm an ex-poor boy who was lifted from my root-soil and transplanted into Andover and Harvard. I remain alienated from society. I cannot be grateful. I want to do simple things with my life that have to do with *me*."

"Survival = mental health."

187–188   8. From another continent, greetings!

I'm hurt, but struggling. Right now I'm trying idealism."

188–189   9. "Can you help me on my application for status as a conscientious objector?"

(Lloyd response omitted.)

189–193   "My draft board turned me down—didn't pay any attention to me, in fact. To answer your question: much of your course was intricately connected to my subsequent thinking as I was heading toward some psychological bottom, which I hit the next year. I'm struggling back."

pages
"I am surrounded by expectations. Just let me help somebody."

"Don't let the bastards get you down!"

VII. A Parable

Blindness with eyes make a good combination.

Appendix II:

Postulates of the Obvious

Distinctions exist.

There is no other place to begin. If we are going to make a statement about the obvious we must start with something that is not self-contradictory. That is, the statement itself is comprised of distinctions as it sits there on the page. It is precisely and only these distinctions which enable us to say that it exists. If it were not distinct from the page around it, and if its different parts were not distinct from each other, it would not exist, it would not be obvious to us. We must respect the necessity of starting here and only here, rather than saying, for example, that when something exists it "becomes" distinct. Existence does not in some way precede distinction; any assumption of a precedent existence obscures the obvious and muddles our thoughts away from the clarity of sensation, which is our intimate and merciless experience of existence. It is important that we make as yet no further assumptions about what we "mean" by existence, or about where existence exists. It is not yet important to ask whether sensations occur within us or outside of us, whether they are to be trusted or disparaged, what relationship they bear to "truth," or how we "process" the information sensations give us. The postulate does not say that *we* exist at all, merely that distinctions exist.

O NLY distinctions exist.

This statement establishes the identity of distinctions and existence: what exists is only distinct, and what is distinguished only exists. Conversely, lack of distinction is identical to lack of existence, and vice versa. Beyond its definitive function, this postulate also implies some important corollaries:

a. So long as there is existence there is distinction; existence within itself is an infinite collection of distinctions; the more we look (invite sensation), the more we see (experience distinction).

b. Therefore when we are talking about something other than an infinitely expanding collection of distinctions, we are talking about something other than existence.

c. The relationship of different parts of existence to each other is *only* one of distinction; within existence no other kind of relationship can be found.

d. Therefore any other kind of relationship that comes forward to us involves something other than existence; existence does not involve or contain logical, aesthetic, causal, coherent, sensible, orderly, evolutionary, revolutionary, economic, theological, sexual, geometric, spatial, temporal, relativistic, physical, geological, astronomical, chemical, biological, historical, geographical, political, linguistic, unconscious, emotional, interpersonal, administrative, structural, functional, meaningful, sociological, psychological, astrological, medical, physiological, educational, mystical, verbal, intellectual, familial, extrasensory, developmental, or scalar relationships, or any other kind of relationship you may mention or invent. Distinction is not itself a relationship but an absence of relationship: whatever are the two things that have been distinguished by a distinction, they can be said to "belong" to each other only as they act to distinguish each other.

ABSENCE of distinctions is identity.

This is more than a definition: the first word postulates "absence," a difficult because peculiarly meaningless interjection. To remain meaningless is its goal, for if "absence" assumes any meaning it assumes a presence and becomes distinct from other presences. Essentially I am trying to establish reference, via the words "absence" and "identity," to what does not exist, to what is not distinct. This is a major step because paradoxical: the two words are distinct and yet are said to refer to something which is other and not at all distinct. The existence of the paradox is obvious, as is the demand it places upon us. Essentially what is interjected here, via the paradox, is a *question,* which is actually *a state of our being.* In other words, when we postulate absence we create questioning by creating a presence which will always suggest its (and our) appearance from nothing or disappearance into nothing.

So far I have left out any questions or statements about thought itself, and will do so for as long as I can, primarily because it is sloppy to think about thought prior to defining some basis for thought. After all, we are already thinking here, and we do not have to worry about what we are doing so long as we can continue. To stop and think about thought would be, at this point, like opening the oven to see if the cake has fallen and so causing it to fall.

IDENTITY does not exist.

Following directly from the first three postulates. More interesting is the intensification of the question: if identity does

not exist, then what does the word "identity" "mean"? The word
and its meaning are clearly different, and yet their relationship is
not referential. In this context, the word "identity" is not a sign
or symbol standing for something else—it stands for nothing,
most particularly for nothing else. Among words, this is exceptional. If the word "identity" refers to nothing else, one might be
tempted to say that it therefore refers only to itself, but this is
nonsense. The word "identity" is obviously not nothing, is distinct and therefore exists. I am suggesting, then, that something
which exists has some special relationship to nothing, or to the
absence of existence. What is brought into question is not the nature of this relationship, which obviously cannot be demonstrated (the bridegroom, or meaning, would never appear at the
church), but our perception of the relationship. How can we perceive nothing, much less name it? Are we stupid when we give it
a name and thereby introduce the paradox facing us? Perhaps we
are. Let us set aside the possibility of stupidity at this point, perhaps to return to it.

ALL nothing is identical.
        That is, one cannot distinguish between nothings: there
are not different kinds of nothing, or different locations, or different times. Does this mean that there is only one Nothing? No,
for this would be to suggest the comparison or contrast of a single nothing with one, two, or more of something else. This postulate reinforces the exclusivity of the relationship between
"identity" and "nothing." It also serves warning: *all that is not
distinguishable is the same.* This may be obvious, but it is
equally obvious that the injunction is often ignored, for example,
whenever we ascribe some special or unique quality beyond what
is distinguishable and so land ourselves in the realm of
superstition—however educated or sophisticated our company. A
homely example: if you have lost something and wish to find it,
you may instigate a procedure of remembering where you have
been, what you were doing with the object, and otherwise try to
reason your way into finding it. But there is a more basic as-

sumption you must make if your search is to be successful: the fact that you do not know where the object is means, equally, that you do not know where it isn't, and your attempts to be reasonable are, at best, a pretense, a form of self-deception, and can often lead you astray. Since you do not know where it is or isn't, it may be anywhere or everywhere. The successful searcher is he who confronts his ignorance totally, operates with the minimal assumptions, and regards with distrust (and total lack of expectations) the few assumptions he must make in order simply to start moving. After that, the issue is to stay open to all sensations, that the object may become distinct when he sees it.

DISTINCTION is neither distinct from nor identical with identity.

Here arises a new problem, that of the relationship between distinction and identity. Do they in any way belong to each other? The postulate seems in some ways contradictory to the exclusivity that has been assigned to each. In effect, the postulate says that the relationship between distinction and identity neither exists (is not distinct) nor is nothing (is not identical). We are further involved in the problem of absence—more particularly, what is its relationship to presence? In fact, this question is central to our further considerations, a major theme of any investigation of the obvious. Let me restate the postulate: something cannot be distinguished from nothing because (as I have suggested before) nothing is not open to an act of distinction. On the other hand, it is axiomatic that something (anything) is not nothing. The strictness of the exclusivity between distinction and identity forces upon us the recognition of the centrality, vitality, and strength of their relationship. This relationship is not simply one of mutual definition—a fact emphasized by this last postulate—but of mutual life, of their necessity to us. But before I lay before you some evidence of this life, let me observe that we are here involved in a problem of the nonexcluded middle. It seems fair to say that two things are either distinct or identical, and yet (if we trust our progress so far) it also seems impossible to so restrict ourselves. As a matter of fact, most things we compare are perceived as neither completely one nor completely the other. Can distinction and identity be stirred together like so much soup? Or perhaps they are mutually repellent, and cannot be brought into contact with each other?

We need to make an effort now to explain how distinction and identity are both different and related. What makes us recognize their absolute difference, and what makes us say that they do indeed have any relationship whatsoever? How can we perceive that two different things are distinct and yet belong to each other?

Absence is not presence. This seems simple enough, and yet we have such great difficulty in coping with absence. Perhaps it is simply that we cannot think about it without making something else become present: thoughts, visions, remembrances, hopes, or understandings crowd in upon us as if to compensate for that utter loss of whatever is or has become utterly absent. What is or has once been distinct lapses into identity, into the same, reminding us of our own personal "time's arrow," our own perceptual entropy. What has become absent is beyond recall, beyond recognition, beyond even supposition. And what has not yet even been absent is beyond imagination—one may even hear faint echoes of laughter at our efforts to picture that doubly removed shadow, whatever will still remain absent whenever or whatever future distinctions become present to us. Our major perceptual clue as to the difference between distinction and identity is simply the fact that distinctions appear and disappear, and if we respect our senses and the differences they bring to us, we know that presence is decidedly different from absence: the more that we make of presence, the more different absence becomes. The more the present is constantly with us, constantly changing, the more drastically it is left behind. Let me stress here that by "absence" I do not mean anything we are thinking about or even mooning over (as in "absence makes the heart grow fonder"), but precisely what we are *not* thinking about or in any other way aware of. If existence is an infinite field of distinction, of presence, then the difference between existence and identity—between existence and absence—is, at least on the side of existence, infinitely varied. That from which identity is absent is infinitely large. There is no special category of existence from which identity is more different. All distinctions are equally nonidentical.

What of the relationship between identity and distinction? As I have stressed, there is no demonstrable connection or belongingness between them. Although, by the desire for immediate consistency, I was forced to start this train of postulates with the existence of distinction, this does not mean that distinction in any way precedes identity. In fact, the absence of the postulate preceded the postulate, and so might be said to have "caused" it in some way. And yet, by the drastic nature of the difference between identity and distinction we are led to question whether the precedence is at all relevant to the question. What happens if we try the reverse? Suppose we "remove" distinction and see what happens to identity, and then "remove" identity and see what happens to distinction.

If there were no distinctions, no existence, would we simply be left with nothing, with distilled identity? We do not, cannot know. But we would not be left with identity *as we know it,* because our knowledge exists. The identity that we have been speaking of so far, *that* identity would not remain because it has become absence for us only via the presence of something else—in this particular case you, me, and some words on a page. Presence of some kind is, for you or for me, necessary for us to contemplate absence. Following from my statement above concerning the quality of all distinctions vis-à-vis identity, it would seem that the number, or quality, or kind of distinctions necessary for our contemplation of identity can vary without changing that necessity—the basic claim which (*for us*) distinction has on identity.

What would happen if we "removed" identity—if we removed the idea of absence from our contemplation of existence? That is, what would happen—either to us or to existence—if we insisted to ourselves that this infinite field of distinctions is complete, is sufficient for our understanding of the world? First, concerning our "understanding," we would be forced to give up any sense of connection between it, as a set of mental distinctions, and whatever else it pretended to explain. We would be forced to admit that even as existence contains only an increasingly large number of distinctions, so we are increasingly distinct from our environs, and in fact, increasingly distinct from ourselves. Indeed, "we" could not be a recognized concept. An alternative would be the espousal of the completeness and self-sufficiency of existence which would proceed by attempting to make equivalent to it, and equally self-sufficient, our understanding, and yet this procedure implicitly uses absence at every step along the way. Such profound (and sometimes arrogant) rationalism constantly subtracts, abstracts, and otherwise throws away evidence (as negligible) without seriously asking itself where those distinctions that have arisen and are then ignored disappear to. The acts of forgetting, ignoring, and suppressing are basic to the rational process, and to any mental or physical act as well, and in fact we could make no sense at all of anything without these uses of absence. Every time we say that some distinction or other "makes no difference" we are in effect saying that we already in some way know something, and can trust our basis of discard. Further, every act of contemplation is based on the supposition that an act of forgetting or setting aside is not a drastic loss or irretrievable step; that somehow the abyss of absence is really friendly, or at least neutral, territory; that its emptiness is not antagonistic. Absence is in some vital way home: it is where we have come from and where, when we return, we will have to be taken in. Such is the claim that identity makes on us and on our experience of the distinctions of existence, even when we are being our most hardheaded and nonsuperstitious. Although it is impossible to make absence present, our most vehement efforts cannot make absence any *more* absent than it already is.

D ISTINCTION is complementary to identity.

We now have a name for the relationship discussed in the last postulate, and the name brings with it the need for further definition and a host of implications. Definition first:

A is complementary to A' if, and only if:

1. A' is complementary to A;
2. A contains no A';
3. The existence of A necessitates the existence of A', and the nonexistence of A necessitates the nonexistence of A';
4. A and A' together form a whole which contains nothing but A and A';
5. The whole which the two form is undefinable except in terms of the two complements which form it: when they do not exist, it does not exist;
6. If, within the whole in which A and A' exist, A changes, A' also changes, at the same time.

Even though there may be some redundancy in this definition, there are also quite a few new considerations which will take some time to unravel:

1. All this first qualification means is that, in the subsequent parts of the definition, one should be able to interchange A and A'. In this case, I have already hinted at the interchangeability of distinction and identity in speaking of the lack of precedence either has over the other. They are totally mutual.

2. This aspect has been well covered by definition.

3. Here we run into some problems. Whereas in the definition, existence (of A) is coupled with existence (of A'), and nonexistence is likewise coupled with nonexistence, in the case of distinction and identity the one is defined as existence *per se* and therefore cannot be said to not-exist, and the other is defined as nonexistence *per se* and cannot be said to exist. Existence can only exist, and identity can only not-exist. We cannot say, then, that the existence of existence necessitates the existence of nonexistence (the presence of identity). Identity can never be present. Nor can existence ever be said to be absent. How is the definition applicable? More important, how does it inform us? We are forced to recognize our own role as mediators of the meaning of the definition, and that the definition is a statement about our mediation rather than about distinction and identity. In other words, to expand the definition to include our mediation, it

would say:

The existence of existence necessitates our continual nonawareness of that which is absent (= our participation with absence), and the removal of existence (although unthinkable) would remove absence as a source of significance for us.

4. The question, long delayed, is: what is the whole which absence and presence—identity and distinction—together form? Most simply stated, this whole is the totality of being, all that *is*, provided that the whole is perceived by the whole of our being. Present to us with the realization of this relationship is the realization of the character of our being, its limits, and its forms of power: the two poles of identity and distinction, neither ever isolable for skeptical scrutiny (and even never present), define the ingredients of being, attested to by the variety in all distinct existence, and by the suggestive hiding of identity. But perhaps you are not ready to accept this definition of being? Perhaps you would insist that this world and universe are inhabited by many things, organisms, and people, the shadows of which are at this very moment floating in your mind, and which have no connection with these elusive and apparently abstract principles? It is my object [1] to solidify those connections and to demonstrate the usefulness—to us—of starting here. Indeed, I hope to show how we do already use them, or are used by them. For the time being will it suffice to reform our statement in this way?

All being is comprised of what we sense together with what we do not sense.

I hope that by this time it is clear that I am trying to remove all metaphysical, epistemological, etiological, theological, or ontological assumptions from the incipient discussion. All I have tried to say so far is that existence—the presence of distinction— is undeniable, and to show that presence forces us to acknowledge absence. The two together form what we can securely involve our thoughts with.

5. There are two parts to this proviso. First, it states that when we speak of "being," we refer only to what is comprised of distinction and identity together, and not to either alone or to

[1] In this book as a whole.

some other completely different idea. The second part refers again to the unthinkable, to the absence of being. If you restrict your attention only to what has been presented here, you may be tempted to postulate being (comprised of presence and absence) and absence of being as complementary, too, and so to start synthesizing an endless series of new wholes (being + absence of being = superbeing; superbeing + absence of superbeing = superduperbeing, etc.). Such a step would be frivolous, and would leave meaning behind: essentially a sin against absence. It will be while before we can contemplate the absence of being.

6. We seem beset. Here I am suggesting—in direct contradiction to other things I have said—that identity can in some way "change" if distinction changes. But identity cannot change. As I have said, all nothing is the same. Therefore, the statement is forced to mean that our perception of identity must change. That is, we are again forced to recognize our own mediation and to modify the wording of our definition to accommodate the uniqueness of what we are talking about—and the uniqueness of its relationship to us. If our perception of identity changes, then, true to our definition of being, our being changes. If our being changes, it would seem obvious that being as a whole changes, but this is a deduction that requires further justification. Is our being a part of, a contribution to being as a whole? There is nothing to indicate otherwise. The only way we could say that our being is not part of being as a whole would be to consign ourselves to absence—that complementary part of being that is not present. Can we say that we are not present? That is, can we say that we (I, you, he, she) are not distinct? No. We cannot say that there is no distinction that we possess or are possessed by. That is (and I must be careful), since I cannot distinguish between the distinctions I perceive and whatever it is that "I" refers to, and since I must say that distinctions exist, I must equally attest to my being. Pushing the necessity of mediation to a personal immediacy, the original question becomes modified:

What basis can I find for the perception that as I move into my future and participate in an increasing variety of presentness my perception of all that is absent changes?

The question is not meant to suggest that my perception of absence is an illusion or some other extrapolated mental operation based on an extrapolated understanding of what I am talking about. Rather, it is meant (again!) to direct your attention to the problematic relationship between presence and absence, specifically the relationship that I can perceive and cannot explain. The only alternative is to say that my perceptions are only an illusion, and that there is "really" no relationship at all between what is present and what is absent. Try as I may, I cannot begin to entertain this possibility. In order to do so I must cease to exist. It seems, then, that the function of our mediation, of our being in being, is precisely to allow us to participate with absence, even though it does not exist. Further, we must never forget this problem, we must never cease to raise the question of our perception of absence, because it is *this* perception (and no other) which relates us—or the absence within us [2]—to all that is (absent) outside us. *All nothing is the same.* My existence forces me to perceive my being, and my being, in turn, forces me to perceive the being of all else.

$$D_{\text{ISTINCTION}}$$ and identity, as complements, together form being, which is neither disjoined nor uniform.

Being is weighted neither toward distinction nor toward identity. The negativity of the postulate points to the difficulty—never entirely absent—of their relationship, and our difficulty in understanding how we, as mediators, derive our life from them. This difficulty is, *per se,* our intellectual life, insoluble and productive. We can never make static or consciously stable, in our minds, a picture or image of the truth of our mediated being without creating the necessity of moving on. We both change and do not change, and somehow our life derives from that paradox, along with our capacity to understand, our sense of significance, our ability to share humanity, and our willingness to move ahead.

If being is neither disjoined nor uniform, what is it? Can we

---

[2] Our internal transparency.

affirm anything beyond that negative statement? Can we say
something that will, without deception, further inform us about
being? Yes, but it is difficult. Being careful about what we say is
not enough: we cannot guarantee truth merely by not telling lies.
The truth here is that this definition of being, despite the absolute definition of its components, is incomplete. The definition
gives no shape to being, no clear correspondance between the
words and our perception of being. We have been walking backward, avoiding the moment when we would have to turn around
and look being in the face, in the eyes. That moment has come.

What do I see when I confront being and stare it in the face? I
see arrivals and departures, density and thinness, richness and
poverty, ebbing and flowing, deceit and honesty, all demanding
concern—a response of my being—and all responding to it. But
more important, I find a unique comfort in the presence of
others—other people, other things—who share my paradoxical
state of change, no-change. Shall I distrust this comfort, this excitement, this vitality I feel in the presence of a person whose
every surprise reminds me of his and my identity, and whose
every consistency is surprising, a source of renewed and unexpected joy? I can find no twinge of suspicion within me which
stands equal scrutiny, nor any reason to fall back in distrust.
Such a person (or thing) convinces me that *he is,* and that *I am*
along with him. Other responses are feeble.

How am I to understand this presence of the being of another,
this strange, living mixture of presence and absence, his changing
existence and his constant partaking, along with me, of an indis-
tinct and essential nothingness? I grope toward understanding
and as I grope my perception becomes bound to him by some
gravity, some curvature of his existence centering on a space, an
unreachable emptiness, a hollow place toward which I turn my
inward eye—blindness staring at blackness—and *see* what he is
to me. And there springs into being what I am to him.

The more distinct his existence, the more hidden his center.
The more dynamic his presence, the more enduring his absence.
Yet the strength of his being is the strength of these mutually exclusive opposites as they come forward and recede, together and
at the same time.

By what right and by what means do I locate him?

By what right and by what means do I attribute existence to him and separate his distinction from all other existence?

These questions are transformed by recognizing and accepting my perception that I *do* locate him and separate him, just as you do. Transformed, they become:

Can I trust my perception that he—this person I confront— has a location?

Can I trust my perception that his existence belongs to him, is centered in him, and has a relationship to him different from its relationship with all other existence?

It is precisely here that we must turn our backs on "explanation," on any resort to subtractive reasoning, on any translation of our mutual sense of integrity into a statement about the "association" of certain "dominant" or "consistent" aspects of his existence which somehow or other convince us that the variety which his existence shows is held together "by" certain characteristics of that existence. Existence does not hold itself together: it constantly diverges and only diverges. Existence is held together by nothing—that is, by identity. To substitute an explanation for the clear perception of this paradox is a form of surrender, and must assume the guilt of gossip.

I am saying that being partakes of two nonfinite referents, distinction and identity (everything and nothing), and yet is finite. Untamed darkness links with untamed light, and the result is granular rather than gray. We perceive that this person we confront is possessive, contained, concretely enjoyable, full of surprises and possibility, "trailing clouds of glory." And we do not know why. We can ask why, and even attempt to answer, but every answer is a lie because every answer is simply an attempt to push the problem under water in the hopes that it will drown. But even the water partakes of being and so will not be an accomplice. The problem floats to the surface, perhaps in another place, alive and kicking. We cannot will this person dead to us by substituting our thoughts for him in his place: thoughts remain only (if superbly) thoughts, and he continues in his evolutionary being, whether or not we wish or partake.

In my relationship to him I have a choice, constantly reiterated, between assumptions of identity and sensations of separation. And, corresponding to the choice, I participate via my perceptions in both. The result is dynamic, bringing him into being for me at the same time as I come into being for him, only in a different way. Because of the difference in our ways, each of us—if we are true to our perceptions on each other—also perceives and partakes in the totality of being, again each in his different way. With the reiterated choice we have toward each other comes reiterated difficulty. Each of us will never be allowed to remain satisfied with an idea of the other because neither of us will allow it. What we can share is not satisfaction. Nor is it distrust. We share our being, with each other and all else.

IN summary:

1. Distinctions exist.
2. Only distinctions exist.
3. Absence of distinctions is identity.
4. Identity does not exist.
5. All nothing is identical.
6. Distinction is neither distinct from nor identical with identity.
7. Distinction is complementary to identity.
8. Distinction and identity, as complements, together form being, which is neither disjoined nor uniform.

Appendix III:
Outline of Thoughts about Personal Survival in Society
(See page 160.)

I. Rationality and Perceptual Politics: Survival in the world of Opinion

> R1: The appeal to reason is an act of compromise and therefore is an appeal for the vote of the majority: generalized thought enlisted in the aid of personal purpose. Be wary.

> R2: Rationality is an act of creation, and systematic thought is a gift: idea becomes thing, permanently useful in our experience and no clear source of threat. Some ideas are trustworthy.

> PP1: Perception is seen as a real variable among people. Different people have different perceptions of reality, and

each must be allowed to trust his own: what else can he trust so well: Perceptual freedom is the basis of our political freedom, whence all blessings flow.

PP2: The issue of "relevance" is simply a perceptual argument, therefore unresolvable.

PP3: Communication, in order to be significant, must be based on perception of reality. Other forms of communication degenerate into messages only.

PP4: Propaganda and gossip are insidious attempts to manipulate our perceptions of reality into partiality, and therefore are the enemies of perceptual freedom. Resist them, whatever their source (including yourself).

II. Anticipation and Transaction: The Shape of Participation

A1: Temporal granularity distinguishes, as we discover our lives, the time before an experience, the time of entering an experience, the time during an experience, the time of disengaging from an experience, and an aftermath.

A2: Preparing to pay attention and to guess intentions is a clear demand and provides unexpected rewards both from another's effort and from our own.

A3: Real questions are not answered in a hurry. Our goal is not to have them answered but to experience them whole.

T1: Contracts are not simply burdens to be born or protection against error and greed: they also express intention and the pleasures of trust.

T2: Being honest is a synthetic activity, truth is a synthetic product, just as being actual is a synthetic state. Therefore, honesty if not easy nor dishonesty difficult.

T3: The person to trust is the honest person, but the experience will be mutually demanding.

T4: To declare a transaction completed is not to forget that the obligation ever existed.

III. Hiding and Display: The Survival of Personality

H1: Dreams occur in the dark.

H2: Unrecognized and unrewarded contributions are still real and therefore valuable: to be meek and noncompetitive is not necessarily to be a sucker.

D1: Credentials are a problem of mutuality. In presenting your credentials, base them always in your totality, your actuality, your honesty, and your hiddenness: credentials are not revealed but constructed.

D2: Preaching and practicing—saying and doing—are not to be confused. The charge of hypocrisy cannot be leveled at the person whose actions improve on his words.

D3: "Authenticity" (a popular word) is the public demonstration of actuality. When something actual enters the imaginary world of society, obvious problems attend: oil and water do not easily mix.

IV. Sacrifice and Overprotection: The Tactics and Transactions of Survival

S1: The complementary aspects of change are creation and destruction. Creation is the establishment of a finite, mediate, and therefore useful distance between two entities; destruction occurs as that distance becomes irreversibly very large or very small.

S2: Actual sacrifices include: forgetting, becoming stupid, losing dreams, becoming tired, exposing oneself to inefficient social friction, the relinquishment of alternative courses of action, and even the personal commitment to a single task which could be called the consumption of self. The ability to slam the door tight on the past is often essential.

S3: Thought of metaphorically, entropy—the tendency for differences to disappear and all to become the same—can describe our experience of loss, or rather, of consumption. We live by a process of removing the differences between things. Therefore, we must see our tendencies toward uniformity both as a loss of life and a gain of living. To enter, for example, into a new habit of thought or behavior is to create a new pattern on which we can rely, but which, as it enters our internal transparency, is necessarily forgotten. What is forgotten is gone. Therefore, make maximum use of all learning as it happens, before it is lost.

O1: Any job, up to and including the entire job of living (of surviving) will require unpredictable resources. The more resources you have absorbed—the more learning you have lived through and forgotten—the more you can depend on yourself. Do not demand narrow proofs of the usefulness of what anybody, including yourself, knows.

O2: Being somewhere and doing something is not to be in a hurry to get elsewhere, but every activity in which you participate and to which you lend yourself should, in addition, build toward another place to be and another thing to do: your environment and your content should always be larger than any particular action or set of actions.

O3: Remember that you are large and many-sided: let no man define you to yourself, or tell you that you have failed.

O4: The transparency of your immediate surroundings and your own hiddenness demands redundant effort: you will have to repeat many jobs, and your gestures will be swallowed up as if never made. Yet a difference will have been made.

V. Afterword: The Morality of Survival

M1: Every person is a gift to the world.

M2: Being given to the world does not mean for you, that all privileges are automatic.

M3: There are standards neither of generosity nor of stinginess. The important thing is what you do, not what somebody thinks you have done—survival, not style.